STONE COLD

Joe Standerline

based on the novel by Robert Swindells

Series Editor: Andy Kempe

STANLEY THORNES (PUBLISHERS) LTD

Original novel © Robert Swindells 1993
Dramatic adaptation © Joe Standerline 1999
Introduction and activities © Andy Kempe 1999

Stone Cold first published in 1993 by Hamish Hamilton

Cover illustration by Martin Berry

Typestyled by Peter Nickol

The right of Joe Standerline to be identified as author of this work
has been asserted by him in accordance with the Copyright,
Designs and Patents Act 1988.

This dramatic adaptation first published in 1999 by:
Stanley Thornes (Publishers) Ltd
Ellenborough House
Wellington Street
CHELTENHAM GL50 1YW
England

99 00 01 02 03/ 10 9 8 7 6 5 4 3 2 1

A catalogue record for this book is available from the British
Library.

ISBN 0-7487-4060-0

Printed and bound in Great Britain by T.J.International Ltd,
Padstow, Cornwall

C O N T E N T S

ACKNOWLEDGEMENTS

Joe Standerline wishes to acknowledge those at Nugent House School who were involved with him in the adaptation of *Stone Cold* for the stage.

In script-writing: James Ashworth, Billy Barnes, Graham Bethell, Steve Burrowes, Jason Cox, Shelagh Halliwell, Mark Heaps, Mark Jameson, Gareth Jones, David Kirkham, Paul Nightingale, Jason Reed, Gareth Robinson, Gary Wade, Lawrence Wood.

In performing, direction and production, and stage and set design: James Ashworth, Billy Barnes, Steve Burrowes, Ian Conners, Daniel Cumbo, Alan Gorman, Shelagh Halliwell, Gary Hughes, Laura Knockton, Gemma Matthews, Lawrence McGinn, Paul Mcloughlan, Phillip Mitchell, Anne Quirk, Peter Walker, Lawrence Wood.

All royalties on sales of this title will be paid to Centrepoint.

SuperScripts

SuperScripts is a series of plays for use in the English classroom and the Drama Studio. The plays have been written by professional writers who share a delight in live performance and the challenges it offers to actors, designers, directors and, of course, audiences.

Most of the plays in the series were written for professional companies. All are included because they tell stories and use techniques which will interest, excite and offer new insights to young people who are just coming to understand how drama works as an art form.

The range of plays in the series addresses the requirement to give students at Key Stages 3 and 4 an opportunity to study a variety of dramatic genres. The fact that they were all written for performance (and have indeed all been performed) means that they will give students the chance to understand how and why playscripts are different from novels. The Activities presented after the script are designed to draw attention to this, and extend students' abilities in reading, writing and of course performing drama.

Many of the tasks invite students to engage directly with the text or formulate their own creative responses. Others focus on discussing, writing and designing. Both English and Drama specialists will find the series a valuable resource for promoting dramatic literacy – and simply performing the plays wouldn't be a bad thing either!

Stone Cold

Centrepoint is a charity that helps homeless young people. They estimate that in London alone there are some 50,000 young people between the ages of 16 and 19 living on the streets. While this fact on its own is shocking enough, simply quoting statistics doesn't always seem a very effective way of changing things. Nor do lists of facts and figures make particularly good drama!

A good story well told, however, can make a considerable impact on society because of the way it translates the facts into personal stories. A good example of this was the television drama *Cathy Come Home* which, when it was first shown in the 1960s, led to debates in Parliament and the establishment of the charity Shelter. Thirty years on, though, it is clear that there are still tragic personal stories unfolding on the streets every day that may serve as a timely reminder that the problems have not been solved.

This play is based on Robert Swindells' novel of the same name. When this was published in 1993, it made an immediate impact and won the Carnegie Award for Children's Literature. One of its great strengths lies in the way it avoids preaching about the plight of all homeless young people, in favour of telling the story of just one person. Although Link can be seen as representing all of the young and homeless, he is not a simple stereotype. He has his own particular personal history, his own fears and desires and certainly his own failings. Perhaps he might have made other choices and taken a different road. But once he sets off on the one he *does* take, the combination of his naivety and the evil that preys on those left to fend for themselves leads to a situation which seems almost inevitable.

That the villain of the piece adopts the name of a charity aimed at helping the homeless emphasises how callousness grows if left unchecked.

In his dramatisation, Joe Standerline has remained true to his original source. Like the novel, the play is deeply moving but also terrifying, building to a sickening climax. But Joe clearly recognises that plays use different tricks to engage an audience. The true identity of Gail, for example, is only revealed at the very end of the novel (which is told in the first person); in the play the audience knows from the outset what Link doesn't. This adds to the dramatic irony of the story and creates an added tension for the theatre audience. The use of short scenes, projected images, voice-overs and direct address makes the play of *Stone Cold* an exhilarating piece of theatre. In this, the script provides a model for exploring how plays are different from novels.

The script of *Stone Cold* developed from a project Joe Standerline undertook with the pupils of Nugent House School on Merseyside, a residential school for boys. Joe writes:

Many of those staying there have had more to endure in their lives so far than most of us would care to think about. One night, one of the boys lay in bed reading the novel Stone Cold. It made such an impression on him that the following day he asked his English teacher if they could turn the book into a play. Not too long after this I came into the frame. It was my job to show them how to come up with the necessary script. I sincerely hope my re-drafting of their ideas does justice not only to Robert Swindell's excellent novel, but to the collective voice of all those involved, and the vision Gareth Jones had while reading late that night.

STONE COLD

C A S T   L I S T

(In order of appearance)

LINK	(real name Dave) 16 years old; son to Joan, stepson to Vince, brother to Carol
SHELTER	In his early forties; one serious head case; thrown out of the army for being out of control
MR GREENWOOD	Link's old teacher
CAROL	Link's sister
JOAN	Link and Carol's mum
VINCE	Joan's boyfriend; lives with her
LOUISE/GAIL	A young reporter who goes 'under cover'
GAVIN	Newspaper photographer; boyfriend to Louise
MIKE	Carol's boyfriend
MR STAMP	Newspaper editor; Louise's boss
ANNOUNCER	
LANDLORD	
TOM	
TOILET ATTENDANT	
PASSER-BY	*(Act 1 Scene 12)*
SCOUSE	
DEBS	
GINGER	17 years old; a friend to Link
PEDESTRIAN 1	
PEDESTRIAN 2	
POLICEMAN	
WAITER	

Passer-by	*(Act 1 Scene 14)*
Bus Queuer 1	
Bus Queuer 2	
Shoppers	*(Act 1 Scene 15: includes* Woman *and* Man*)*
Trina	A benefit officer
Toya	
Greg	
Hook	A neighbour of Shelter's; runs a hostel for the homeless
Dosser	*(Act 1 Scene 16)*
Chorus of dossers	
8 dossers	*(Act 2 Scene 2)*
Nick	A *Big Issue* seller
Cafe owner	
Businessman	
Businessman 2	
Man	*(Act 2 Scene 6)*
Bouncer	
Middle-aged man	Toya's father
Police 1	(female)
Police 2	(male)

ACT ONE

SCENE 1

The street. A litter bin. A yellow spot comes up on
***Link**. He looks bored. His clothes are scruffy and he
looks dirty. He takes a good look at the audience
then speaks to them.*

LINK   Have you ever sat and watched people, really
watched them? They're all in their own little world.
Now and then they'll let you in, if they're feeling
brave or if they think they know you. But the rest of
the time you might as well be invisible.

*A couple of passers-by walk straight in front of him.
One drops a crisp packet at his feet.*

See what I mean.

***Link** picks up the crisp packet and looks to see if
there's anything left inside. There isn't. He moves
towards the litter bin. The lights fade.*

SCENE 2

***Shelter's** living room. There is an arm chair, small
table, standard lamp and fire place. A doorway leads
from this room to the bathroom and kitchen. There is
a window with heavy, drawn curtains. A cat lies
quietly in a basket in front of the fireplace. Above is
hung a portrait of an old-looking soldier. **Shelter**
enters with a bowl of tomato soup.*

SHELTER   *(Thinking out loud.)* Haven? … Home… House…

*He sits down, puts his soup on the table and picks up
a dictaphone and starts to record.*

Day One. Everything is ready. Practice mission
executed successfully. Executed. *(Sniggers. There's a
knock at door; **Shelter** ignores it.)* Only complaint at
present time is constant pestering from man

upstairs. Have now verified code name and will shortly post mission statement to relevant body. Operation to be known as...

He stops the tape for time to think. He ignores another knock at the door.

Hostel? ... Shack? ... Shed? ...

Another knock, he is slightly riled.

Shelter! That's it. (*Recording it.*) Operation Shelter! Perfect. Succinct yet welcoming.

Switches the tape off and slurps a mouthful of soup. There's another knock, the soup drips from his mouth as he speaks.

Get. Lost.

He sits at the table and starts to write. Lights snap back to the street scene.

SCENE 3

The street

LINK Wish I *had* been invisible this afternoon though.

Mr Greenwood appears in a spotlight. He peers forward, as if looking at Link.

Mr Greenwood, my old geography teacher. Last time he saw me was in school, picking up my GCSE certificates. That was a couple of months ago now. Today, I was picking a half eaten bag of chips out of a rubbish bin ...

Link puts the crisp packet in the bin.

He just stared at me at first. I wanted the ground to swallow me up. He started to make his way over.

MR GREENWOOD Are you who I think you are?

LINK I tried to ignore him. I twisted my face up a bit

	hoping he'd mistake me for a stranger.
MR GREENWOOD	David?
LINK	(*Facing forward, as if talking to **Mr. Greenwood**.*) You've got the wrong bloke mate sorry.
MR GREENWOOD	Hey, this is me you're talking to. Why don't you let me buy you a coffee, you look as though you could do with it.
LINK	(*Trying to disguise his voice.*) Me mam told me not to go off with strangers.
	Pause
MR GREENWOOD	I'm sorry, you just look like someone I... (*Takes change from his pocket. Offers it forward. **Link** relaxes a little.*) Please take it. Buy yourself some chips.
LINK	No I'm fine.
MR GREENWOOD	Are you sure?
LINK	Yes Sir!
	*Link winces, realising he's given the game away. Lights fades on **Mr. Greenwood**.*
LINK	I've thought about going home but that would mean apologising. (*Pause.*) My mam used to live for us when it was just me, my sister Carol, and her. Nothing else mattered. Until she met Vince.
	Carol and Joan appear on another part of the stage.
CAROL	...you're just too scared to admit it. I hate him, I really hate him. He's disgusting.
JOAN	Come on Carol love, he doesn't deserve that.
CAROL	So you're still denying it then?
JOAN	Denying what?
CAROL	The fact that your fancy man has been trying it on with your own...

15

JOAN Now that's enough. It's about time you grew up a bit...(*Carol* tries to interrupt.) I didn't ask yer dad to run off, Carol, if it were up to me he'd still be here.

CAROL What's that got to do with it?

JOAN Vince isn't a bad man, love. I know you're upset but you shouldn't be taking it out on him. If you'd just give him a chance...

CAROL You think I'm making it up don't you?

JOAN No love. He did tell me about what happened.

*Pause. **Carol** is stunned.*

CAROL So you already knew what he tried to do?

JOAN Love, it wasn't like that. He asked me to have a word with you about it all. He feels ever so bad.

CAROL Does he.

JOAN It was all a big misunderstanding.

CAROL You've got that much right. I can't believe you're taking his word against that of your own daughter. I'm going. I'm getting out.

JOAN You don't have to do that.

CAROL I think I do.

JOAN He'd had a couple of drinks...

CAROL Leave it out mam please.

*Exit **Carol**.*

JOAN (*Shouting after her.*) He was only trying to have a laugh with you, that's all Carol love.

*Exit **Joan**. Lights back on **Link**. He wonders into the living room space.*

LINK She moved in with her boyfriend after that. With no one to back me up, it was like living in a nightmare.

*Enter **Vince**.*

16

Vince   How old are you?

Link   Don't start.

Vince   I was working when I was your age. Bringing
money home to help pay my way, know what I'm
saying?

Link   No.

Vince   So where have you been?

Link   Stayed at our Carol's.

Vince   Your mother was worried.

Link   Shouldn't have locked me out then should you.

Pause.

Vince   So?

Link   What?

Vince   Where is it? If you're expecting me to keep yer lad
you've got another thing coming. Things have
changed round here. You pay your own way.

Link   How much do you pay?

*Enter **Joan**. She hands **Vince** a mug of tea.*

Joan   You're not arguing again are you Dave?

Vince   What do you think.

Joan   Spoke to our Carol this morning. Why didn't you
tell me you were staying out?

Vince   Cos he's too inconsiderate, that's why.

Joan   If you're not going to come home, you should at
least call…

Link   I did come home. You were still at work. I'd been
locked out

Joan   (*To **Vince**.*) Did you go out love?

Vince   Yes…

LINK	No, cos I could see him through the gap in the curtains when I was hammering on the door.
VINCE	I went out!
LINK	Mam, he didn't. And I tried to call, I was trying nearly all night but it was engaged…
VINCE	Carol put you up to this did she? Part of her 'Chuck Vince On the Street' campaign.
JOAN	Come on Dave.
LINK	I'm telling the truth, mam.
VINCE	(*Pretending to be upset and getting up.*) I'm sorry love, I can't take any more of this.
JOAN	(*Mouthing to* **Link**.) 'Look what you've done.'
VINCE	I have to get out for an hour. Give you and the lad some time together. Erm, have you got…?
JOAN	(*Going for her purse.*) Yeah, hang on.
VINCE	… I'm on your side son, I only wish you'd see it.

Joan hands *Vince* a ten pound note. He takes it, then exits, still trying to look hurt.

SCENE 4

The office of the Daily Tribune. A phone is ringing. Enter **Louise** *being chased by* **Gavin**. *They run around the desk like children.*

LOUISE	I'm going to answer it, stop now.
GAVIN	OK.

Louise is about to pick up the receiver when *Gavin* starts to take photos of her.

LOUISE	(*Trying not to laugh.*) I'm warning you! (*Picks up the phone.*) Good afternoon, Daily Tribune, Louise Bain spea… Oh yes Sir. …I'm supposed to be covering the paper shop incident in Hackney, I was just on

my way in fact...

Gavin fools around, trying to make her laugh.

Do you want me to send someone else?... Yes sir, two minutes... Sorry sir, one minute, yes.

Louise puts the phone down. She looks amazed.

GAVIN   So, what's the good news?

LOUISE   I think I've got an assignment.

GAVIN   Come on cup cake...

LOUISE   He said I'm to forget the Hackney job and go straight to his office for a briefing.

GAVIN   Louise, you haven't been here long enough. No one gets an assignment after that short a time.

LOUISE   Maybe I'm special.

GAVIN   You're special all right.

Exit Gavin and Louise, Gavin chasing her as before.

SCENE 5

Carol's flat. Link is there.

CAROL   So, how've you been then?

LINK   You sound like you haven't seen me for years. It's only been a week.

CAROL   Sorry.

LINK   I'm OK I s'pose. 'least I don't have to look at that swine all day.

CAROL   Not found anywhere to stay yet then?

LINK   No but I've got a couple of ideas. Is it all right if I have a bath again?

CAROL   (*Feeling ashamed.*) Yeah, hurry up mind. Mike'll be back soon and he'll want one himself.

LINK   He doesn't like me coming here does he?

CAROL   It's not that Dave. He just thinks you should be at our mam's.

LINK   You don't have to tell him I've been.

CAROL   It is his flat.

LINK   You wouldn't be here if it wasn't for Vince would yer?

CAROL   Mike's been asking me to move in for ages.

LINK   Do you love him Carol?

CAROL   Are you going to have this bath or not?

LINK   No, you're all right. (*Looks at his watch.*) I've got to meet someone, just remembered.

Link turns away.

CAROL   We're all invited to our mam's for Christmas dinner. Will you come?

Pause

LINK   (*To audience.*) Ever get the feeling you're not wanted? Nine days I've been out here now. That was the third time I'd been to our Carol's. Can't blame her I s'pose.

He positions a few pieces of cardboard on the ground and tries to make himself comfortable.

If someone were to tell me, even a couple of months ago, that I'd be stuck out here on Christmas Eve, I think I'd have laughed in their face.

*A couple of people pass by, giving **Link** a filthy look.*

I'm going somewhere else when I get the cash together. Too many people know me here.

*An up-tempo version of 'Santa Claus is Coming to Town' fades in. Lights cross-fade to show **Vince**, **Joan**,*

Mike and Carol post Christmas dinner. They're wearing paper party hats. The music fades but remains audible.

MIKE   Hey Vince?

VINCE   What?

Mike belches.

Not bad lad, but this un'll be better.

Vince belches.

CAROL   Do you have to?

MIKE   Stop yer moaning woman, Christmas isn't it! *(To Joan.)* Get me and the lad another beer will you love.

Joan gets up. Carol pulls her down again.

CAROL   Let them get it mam.

JOAN   *(Getting up again.)* I don't mind.

Exit Joan.

MIKE   Pull a cracker with us Carol.

CAROL   That's the last one. You should save it.

MIKE   What for, next year?

VINCE   'Ere son. *(Pulls cracker with Mike.)* What's in it?

CAROL   It's a little comb, look.

MIKE   Give that to your Dave then.

Vince and Mike howl with laughter. There is a knock at the door.

CAROL   That's not funny you two.

MIKE   Too touchy, that's your trouble.

Enter Joan and Link.

JOAN   Look who it is.

VINCE	Ah, Stig of the Dump!
JOAN	Vince, don't.
VINCE	Don't what?
JOAN	Sit down love.
CAROL	This is your chair.
VINCE	Yeah, the one covered in plastic.

Vince and Mike snigger. Carol tuts.

MIKE	(*To Carol.*) What's the matter with you today?
VINCE	(*To Link.*) Davey thinks it's funny don't yer lad?
LINK	Hilarious Vince, yeah.
CAROL	Take no notice. It's nice to have you with us Dave. We've got a present for you 'ant we mam?
JOAN	Yeah.
LINK	(*Embarrassed.*) Oh. Great.
VINCE	It's a bar of soap!

More sniggering.

CAROL	Would you fetch it for us please Mike?

Mike gets up reluctantly.

LINK	I don't know what to say. I didn't bring presents for anyone.
JOAN	That's all right son. We know you haven't got much.

Mike finds a large parcel. He begrudgingly hands it to Carol.

CAROL	(*Handing Link the present.*) It's from all of us Dave.
LINK	Thanks.
JOAN	We all put to...
VINCE	I bloody didn't.

CAROL   Thought it might be useful, you know.

Link stands up and starts to open the parcel. He faces front as a sleeping bag rolls out in front of him. It's red and green, reminiscent of Christmas.

LINK   (*Upset, though trying not to show it.*) A sleeping bag. Thanks.

Blackout.

SCENE 6

*Daily Tribune office. **Mr Stamp** on the phone.*

MR STAMP   Gavin, I want to see the shots you got of the bypass this morning... The accident, yes... Bad view? You were in a flaming helicopter Gavin!... Just bring what you've got... Mmm?

*Enter **Louise.***

LOUISE   (*Clears throat.*) You wanted to see me sir?

MR STAMP   ...I just want to look at them, OK? (*Puts phone down. To **Louise**.*) Yeah. Sit down. How long have you been at the Tribune?

LOUISE   Erm, three and...

MR STAMP   Three months?

LOUISE   Three and a half sir...

MR STAMP   Mmm. Big difference. Tell me, what are your thoughts on undercover journalism? ˙

LOUISE   I suppose it would depend on the type of story sir. Why?

MR STAMP   (*Handing over a folder.*) Have a butchers at this.

Louise looks through the file. Phone rings.

Stamp. ...Hold the fort, I'll be down in a second. (*To **Louise**.*) Delivered this morning. Probably a wind up, though being a paper with a responsibility to our gentle readers, I feel we should look into it.

LOUISE   This is... quite threatening.

MR STAMP   Some sad arse looking for attention, I'd say. Still, I'm thinking we might just give him some. (*Gets up.*) Everything's there. Tell me in the morning.

*Exit **Mr Stamp**. **Louise** reads on. Enter **Gavin** with photos.*

GAVIN   We really must stop meeting like this. Is he around?

LOUISE   Hmm?

GAVIN   Stamp.

LOUISE   (*Still looking at the letter.*) Just missed him.

GAVIN   So, he gave you a huge promotion then went to make you coffee, that it?

LOUISE   (*On her way out, still reading.*) Black no sugar thanks.

Lights fade to black.

SCENE 7

A railway station. Announcement chimes are heard.

ANNOUNCER   Bradford Interchange would like to apologise for the delayed 11.30 service from Doncaster. This train is expected to arrive... at some time in the next two hours. Happy New Year.

*Lights up on **Link** and **Carol** standing beneath a platform sign.*

CAROL   How did you pay for the ticket?

LINK   Mam gave me some. Thanks for the lift.

Announcement chimes.

ANNOUNCER   Could passengers waiting for the 13.15 service to London Kings Cross, please make their way to platform four.

LINK   That's me then.

CAROL   Are you sure you know what you're doing Dave?

LINK   Positive.

CAROL   Look after yourself.

LINK   Yeah, you too. I'll come back and see you some day.

CAROL   You'd better.

*There's an uncomfortable pause before they go into a big hug. **Link** is the first to pull away.*

LINK   See yer.

He starts to exit.

CAROL   (*Running after him.*) Dave, wait! (*Handing him an envelope.*)

LINK   What's this?

CAROL   Just take it.

***Carol** pushes the envelope into **Link's** hands. He opens it and takes out several notes.*

LINK   Carol, no. I can't

CAROL   Take it I said.

*Pause while **Link** dithers.*

You'll miss it!

LINK   Thanks sis. Thanks for everything.

*Exit **Link**. **Carol** watches him walk away. She's crying as the lights go down.*

SCENE 8

Shelter's living room. He stands with his dictaphone.

SHELTER (*Sighs.*) Prospect of a very prosperous winter. Charing Cross was full of them. (*Mimicking in a whinging, pathetic voice.*) 'I'm only seventeen, help me please.' I'll help all right. (*Suddenly angry.*) Twenty nine years I fought for the likes of them. What thanks did I get? (*Calms down and puts on a cosy-looking cardigan.*) Time to introduce Mr Shelter. (*Goes into his do-gooder character.*) The warm hearted, 'next door' type, spending all his time helping the miserable little so-and-so's... that are too bloody useless to help themselves. (*Picking up his cat.*) Hello Sappho. (*He pets the cat with genuine affection and becomes himself again.*) Won't have to sleep in doorways soon will they boy, hmm? (*Pointing to the floor.*) Got the perfect place here if they're lucky enough to be recruited.

He laughs. Lights cross-fade to a street. **Link** *is standing in front of a filthy-looking door.*

LINK (*Takes the envelope out and looks at the notes inside.*) One hundred and fifty quid. Get ready London. (*To audience.*) Train got in about three hours ago. First thing I did was to phone some fella up about a bedsit. Had an advert in a shop window. Said I had to be here if I wanted to see it.

*Enter **Landlord**.*

LANDLORD Dave is it?

LINK Oh, yeah. Starting to think I had the wrong place. Landlord right?

LANDLORD (*Opening the door.*) I haven't got all day.

*They go through the door. **Landlord** switches on a dim, bare light.*

LANDLORD (*Pointing.*) Sink. Immersion heater. Lavvy. Bed. Meter. Fifty quid a week, fortnight in advance and that's doing you a favour.

LINK Didn't it say the rent was negotiable in your advert?

LANDLORD All right, sixty pounds a week, three weeks in advance!

LINK I can't afford that!

LANDLORD Fifty then and back to a fortnight.

LINK Er, yeah. I suppose.

LANDLORD There, you've negotiated.

LINK (*Taking his money out.*) So, that makes it...

LANDLORD (*Snatching cash.*) Hundred.

LINK Hundred quid, yeah.

LANDLORD (*Handing him the key.*) Welcome home.

*Exit **Landlord**.*

LINK (*To audience.*) Can't believe it. I've dreamed of having my own place for years, never thought it would be one in London mind. Right, I've fifty quid to tide me over till I get a job sorted.

Light bulb goes off with a clunk.

Where did he say the meter was?

SCENE 9

*Daily Tribune office. **Louise** is trying out different accents.*

LOUISE Hi, my name's Lynn. No, erm, Hi, I'm Fiona.

*Enter **Gavin**.*

The name's Shelagh, you can call me She.

GAVIN Hello She.

LOUISE   (*Shocked.*) Don't do that.

GAVIN   You didn't call me last night.

LOUISE   I was thinking about this assignment.

GAVIN   He's offered this to you because you're the only one on the staff who looks young enough.

LOUISE   And you think I can't handle it, that it?

GAVIN   No. You just don't know what might happen. It could be dangerous.

LOUISE   I could be saving people's lives Gavin.

GAVIN   And risking your own. Don't do it darling.

LOUISE   I've already accepted.

SCENE 10

*The bedsit. **Link** is sitting cross-legged on the floor, eating baked beans from a tin.*

LINK   (*Play-acting.*) 'How was your meal Sir?' 'Delightful thank you waiter.' 'And would Sir like to order a sweet?' 'Not this time thank you, I'm on a diet.'

*Hammering at the door. **Link** jumps up.*

Who is it?

LANDLORD   Room service, who do you think? You going to open the door or shall I use the key?

LINK   (*Opening the door.*) You come to make sure everything's all right?

LANDLORD   Is it?

LINK   I think something's wrong with the meter, it keeps swallowing the coins and nothing happens.

LANDLORD   Pay up and I'll get it looked at.

LINK   But it's Friday!

LANDLORD   I know what day it is.

LINK I moved in on a Monday. I paid two weeks in advance! Don't owe anything till after the weekend.

Landlord pushes his face up against Link's and grinds his teeth.

LANDLORD Listen sunshine, it's me who makes the rules round here and today's rule is, you either pay up or you get out!

LINK You'll get your money. I'm getting my first wages Monday morning. I told the boss I'd need 'em so I could pay you.

LANDLORD Friday is pay day son.

LINK I didn't get the job till Wednesday. He's doing me a favour...

LANDLORD *(Takes the key from Link.)* Nice of him isn't it.

Link is about to plead.

Sling it!

Link grabs his pack and turns to Landlord.

LINK I'll have you for this.

Landlord laughs to himself as light fades.

LINK *(To audience.)* I'll kill him. Be sorry he was ever born, miserable hard-faced... Hundred quid! He must be loaded. *(Slumps down.)* There was me feeling like I'd won the lottery with hundred and fifty quid in me pocket. Now look, I've been here less than a week and all I've got is a sleeping bag, my clothes, fifteen poxy quid and this. *(Takes his watch off and looks at the inscription.)*

JOAN *(Off.)* 'To Dave, the best son in the world'.

LINK Half past eight on a freezing Friday night, somewhere in London and the 'best son in the world' is officially homeless.

SCENE 11

Shelter's room. He has Sappho in his arms, stroking it very gently. He is speaking into his dictaphone.

SHELTER   It's begun. Easy too. Found the first one in a doorway in Camden.

*Places Sappho in his basket. **Shelter** puts on a smart overcoat. Lights cross-fade to a street. **Tom**, the first recruit, is huddled there.*

Bit of a rough night but it takes more than a spot of inclement weather to stop Mr Shelter. Saw it then, shivering like a pathetic little puppy.

*Sits next to **Tom**.*

SHELTER   What's the matter friend, down on your luck?

TOM   Who are you?

SHELTER   (*With a big do-gooder smile.*) They call me Shelter, how about you?

TOM   (*Sarcastically.*) Tom's the name, street life's the game.

SHELTER   Maybe I can help. I run a hostel for people like you.

TOM   (*Unconvinced.*) Great.

SHELTER   Though we're full tonight sadly...

TOM   Not much 'help' then is it?

SHELTER   Why don't you come home with me and make use of the couch? There'll probably be a place at the project tomorrow.

TOM   You must think I was born yesterday. I wouldn't go home with you if you had the last couch in the world. I can smell a pervert a mile off.

SHELTER   Has anything happened to you son? You know, anyone tried anything? You can tell me about it.

Tom   Get a kick out of that would yer?

Shelter   I have a list of known offenders. I'm trying to take some cases to prosecution.

Tom   You a copper then?

Shelter   I run a shelter. I told you. Would you recognise any of your abusers if you saw them again?

Tom   There haven't been any, right.

Shelter   OK. I'm sorry. (*Handing him a card.*) It's the address of the project. Come by tomorrow, I'll see if I can get you a place.

Shelter starts to walk away.

Tom   Happened to a mate of mine though.

Shelter turns back.

Shelter   Would you recognise a photofit, son?

Tom   Maybe.

Shelter   Come on.

Shelter helps Tom to his feet. They exit. Lights cross back to Shelter's room. Tom's coat hangs on the back of the chair. Enter Shelter. He places a bowl of hot soup on the table.

Shelter   (*To audience.*) Too soft for my own good. Poor sod was soaking by the time we got back. So I offered him some nice, hot soup and suggested he had a bath while I prepared it. Didn't cherish the idea of an infested brat using my bathroom. Better than him stinking the place out though.

Enter Tom through joining door. He's wrapped in a huge white towel and drying his hair.

Tom   That was amazing! I can't thank you enough mister.

Shelter   Seeing a young person happy is thanks enough.

Shelter sits Tom in the chair. He hands him the soup.

Here you are lad.

TOM   Thanks. Smells great, what is it?

SHELTER   (*Standing behind the chair.*) Tomato surprise.

TOM   What's the surprise, no tomatoes in it?

SHELTER   (*Fake laugh.*) Ha haar! No lad,

*Shelter lifts a huge knife above **Tom's** head.*

...it's this!

Lights snap to black.

SCENE 12

*Charing Cross Station. Enter **Link** looking for a place to sleep. He spots a doorway and puts his bedroll down.*

LINK   (*Looks at his watch.*) Hardly the Ritz but it'll have to do I suppose. Don't fancy going through that lot again. (*Takes a moment to get comfortable, then starts to fidget.*) I can understand flats being hard to find but you'd think doorways would be easy. This floor's wet. How do they do it, night after night? Feels like I'm sitting on ice. Slowly melting and soaking into the seat of my pants. You get to a point when it feels like your bones are scraping on the concrete. (*Tries to settle again.*) I don't know whether I'm just cold or I need a pee. (*Disappointed.*) I'll wait. (*Pause.*) Nope, don't think I can. (*Stands up, about to pee.*) Bad enough getting treated like an animal, not going to start acting like one. (*Looks around for a suitable place.*) Station!

*Rolls his sleeping bag up, occasionally stopping to cross his legs. Light up to reveal **Toilet Attendant** sitting by a turnstile. He looks asleep. Enter **Passer-by**.*

(*To **Passer-by**.*) Excuse me mate, do you know

where the toilets are?

PASSER-BY (*Pointing towards **Attendant**.*) Just over there.

LINK Cheers. (*He makes his way over. And sees the turnstile.*) Typical! (*Looks at the stile. Rummages through his pockets.*) Ten pence! Come on! Just my luck, a five, two twenties and one pee. (*Crosses his legs.*) Ooh, wish I hadn't said that! (*To sleeping **Attendant**.*) Excuse me! (*No reply.*) Excuse me!!

*Attendant remains oblivious. **Link** throws his bag over the turnstile then jumps after it. He goes just out of view and pees.*

LINK (*Off.*) Aaaaaaahhh!

*Attendant wakes as **Link** re-enters looking relieved. **Attendant** grabs him.*

ATTENDANT 'Ere, have you paid?

LINK No. I haven't got any t...

ATTENDANT I don't give a toss about what you haven't got son.

LINK I just wanted...

ATTENDANT We all 'just want' a lot of things, but most of us believe in paying for them first.

LINK I couldn't.

ATTENDANT You're not leaving my sight until you give me ten pence.

LINK (*Fed up with his attitude.*) Get out of my way you old fart!

*Link throws his bed-roll at the **Attendant** who ducks out of its way.*

Time to leave I think!

*Link picks it up again, then jumps over the stile. 'Eye of the Tiger' fades in. **Attendant** goes to grab **Link**, who threatens to swing a left hook. **Attendant** backs* *away. **Link** runs away. He performs a lap of honour, feeling like a 'champ'. Once back at his doorway, he accidentally kicks something lying there. Music stops suddenly. **Scouse** is lying in the doorway. He gets up in stages (sits, kneels, then stands). He is much bigger than **Link**.*

Oh!

SCOUSE What's your problem lad?

LINK *(Swallows hard.)* Erm, I was here first?

SCOUSE Sod off kidda before I drop yer.

LINK It took me three hours to find this speck, I've just been to the...

SCOUSE *(Prodding **Link** on each word.)* I said sod off!

LINK Come on, you know what it's like, I was here before you honest.

SCOUSE *(Grabbing his wrist.)* Nice watch.

LINK Yeah, and you're not having it.

SCOUSE Yes I am pal. Cos you're going to give it to me. Unless you want to be eating hospital food in precisely... *(Snatches watch)* ...two minutes. *(Looking at watch, now in his hands.)* Tah lah, very nice of you. Now piss off!

***Link** exits while **Scouse** admires his prize. Lights fade as 'Another day in Paradise' by Phil Collins comes up. The following groups of images are projected onto three screens around the stage:*

A 1 *A young-looking Joan holding Link as a baby.*
　 2 *A market trader giving Link an apple.*
　 3 *Link in a doorway, watching a mother with pram and toddler walking past.*

B 1 *Link aged five.*
　 2 *Link walking in a crowded London street.*
　 3 *Link feeding pigeons in Trafalgar Square.*

C 1 Link looking in a rubbish bin with a couple of young girls watching him.
2 Link Looking into the window of a restaurant.
3 Link cross-legged, taken at ground level through the legs of people passing by.

D 1 Link aged ten.
2 Charing Cross station.
3 Link washing in a public toilet with people looking on in disgust.

The montage ends with three pictures of Link in a doorway in different sleeping positions. Music fades out.

SCENE 13

Shelter's room. Military music playing. Shelter enters wearing a smart suit. He opens a trap door in the floor and takes out a large biscuit tin, a Polaroid (or similar) camera and his dictaphone. He takes a photo from the tin then puts the tin and the camera back under the floor.

SHELTER   (*Looking at the photograph while recording.*) Easy as A.B.P! Have ensured no patterns have been formed or followed. That's how a fella gets caught.

Puts the photo down. He delivers the following with military-styled actions.

Change the time.

Change the place.

Change the sex.

And change the race! With those simple rules, not even Cracker could catch me.

Music and lights fade as Shelter puts his coat on and walks onto the street. There's a bus shelter with the entrance to an hotel behind. Debs comes out of the hotel. Shelter creeps from the bus stop and taps her on the shoulder.

SHELTER (*Authoritative.*) Excuse me!

DEBS (*Nervous.*) Yes?

SHELTER Hotel security! I have just followed you.

DEBS (*Frightened.*) I just went in to use the toilet.

SHELTER I've no doubt you are already aware, there has been a series of thefts of late – and we've had you under surveillance. (*Grabbing her by the arm.*) I'm afraid I'll have to ask you to come back into the hotel.

DEBS I didn't take anything. I just went in to use the toilet.

SHELTER This way please.

He drags her in the direction of the hotel. **Debs** *struggles.*

DEBS (*Stopping.*) Look, I'm in enough trouble as it is. I've nowhere to go, no job, no money…

SHELTER (*Changing tack.*) Nowhere to go. Where've you been staying then?

DEBS Different places. Let me go please.

SHELTER Can't be doing that my love, you're a criminal.

DEBS I'm not, I told you.

SHELTER Nasty night tonight don't you think.

DEBS If you say so.

SHELTER I do. (*Suggestive.*) How would you like to spend it in a cosy little apartment? (*Pause.*) Nice warm bed?

DEBS (*Struggling.*) Leave it out. I'm not interested.

SHELTER Just a thought. Might see my way to letting you off the hook if er, …you'd promise to be nice to me?

DEBS Please, let me go. You'll never see me again, I promise. I'll move away.

SHELTER   Nice try. Why don't you come back to the hotel then. Three of my mates are on security tonight.They love a bit of a strip search. Into that sort of thing are you?

No reply.

I said...!

DEBS   No.

SHELTER   Get us a taxi then shall I.

*Lights fade back to **Shelter's** room. He is recording once more.*

SHELTER   It was her own fault. Wonder how many times she'd been told not go with strangers. (*Turns picture to reveal a photo stuck to the back.*) Didn't do anything dishonourable of course. Just told her to get the soup down her neck, then gave it a little twist. (*Picks up the second photo.*) Can see where it snapped if you look closely.

*Looks at the photo, smiles proudly, then sticks it to the back of the picture. Military music fades up again. **Shelter** sings along.*

> There'll always be an England,
> And England will be free,
> Of all the dirty dossers,
> And all because of me!

Fade to black.

SCENE 14

*The street. **Link** is looking for somewhere to sleep. Someone coughs. **Link** tightens his grip on his back pack. He spots a doorway, unrolls his sleeping bag and lies down in it. Enter **Ginger**. Hearing footsteps, **Link** sits up. He sees **Ginger** standing there.*

GINGER   This your speck?

Link gets up in flash. He's afraid but tries not to show it.

LINK   Yes, why?

GINGER   I'm knackered. Mind if I share your doorway?

Link thinks about it while he looks Ginger over.

LINK   No, come on. There's plenty of room.

GINGER   Much more walking about tonight an' I'd have collapsed, haven't eaten since this morning. Thanks mate. (*Sets his make-shift bed next to Link.*) Anyone else would tell me to get knotted.

Pause. Neither can think of anything to say. Link breaks the silence.

LINK   What's your name then?

GINGER   Ginger. That's what my mates call me.

Enter two Pedestrians.

What's yours?

LINK   (*Tries desperately to think of a name.*) Erm...

PED. 1   We're going to be late?

PED. 2   No, we'll be all right. We can get a taxi over by the link-way.

LINK   (*Shouts.*) Link! Yeah, that's it, Link!

Pedestrians spot the two of them and make a swift exit.

GINGER   I heard you the first time.

LINK   (*Taking a Snickers bar from his pocket.*) Sorry. (*Handing it to Ginger.*) Here, do you want this?

GINGER   You sure?

LINK   Yeah, go on.

Ginger takes the Snickers bar and unwraps it

feverishly.

GINGER I'll break it in half.

LINK No, you have it. I'm not hungry.

Ginger starts to chomp at the Snicker. Link watches. It's obvious he's hungry himself. Enter Policeman.

GINGER Ta Link, you just saved my aching belly. What I wouldn't give for a taste of my mum's cooking right now I tell yer.

LINK *(About to cry.)* I'm tired. *(Lies down and rolls away.)* See you in the morning.

Ginger lets out a huge sigh, then lies down himself. The Policeman starts to shine his torch around the stage. The beam sweeps past the lads and then inches back again, picking them out.

POLICEMAN What have we here then?

Goes over to the lads and gives one of them a kick. They both sit up with his torch shining in their faces.

Right, up you get lads. And if you knew what's good for you, you'd get yourselves home.

Link is hurriedly packing his bed away.

GINGER Would if we had homes to go to. *(To Link.)* Who does he think he is?

POLICEMAN A police officer, that's who.

Link and Ginger get up.

POLICEMAN *(Shining his torch on some litter.)* Gonna leave that there are you?

GINGER It's nothing to do with us.

Link picks the rubbish up.

POLICEMAN Get a move on!

Link and Ginger walk on. Exit Policeman.

GINGER   We could've had a cell for the night then. Haven't been round long have you?

LINK   About a day. You?

GINGER   Two.

LINK   Days?

GINGER   Years. And that is a long time to be out here, believe me.

LINK   I need to sleep, my eyes are killing.

GINGER   It's too cold, you'll never get to sleep now. (*Moves away.*) Come on.

LINK   Where you going?

GINGER   Kebab house. Got any money?

LINK   Yeah. About nine pound fifty, how about you?

GINGER   (*Pulling out some coppers.*) Not much. You should keep quiet about how much money you've got you know.

LINK   But you just asked me.

GINGER   Yeah, I know. But don't show off about it. You'll get beaten up and have it taken off you. Understand?

LINK   Yeah.

They walk into the kebab house, comprising a counter, a waiter and two stools.

LINK   I've got to eat something.

GINGER   You said you didn't want anything before.

LINK   That was before. What are you having?… On me.

GINGER   Oh, er… Coffee and a kebab then please.

WAITER   (*To **Link**.*) What about you?

LINK   Same. Thanks.

***Waiter** prepares the food.*

GINGER So where did you get your money from, got a job or something?

LINK Did have, for about a week. This is what's left of the wages.

GINGER Won't last. Especially if you keep buying me grub!

LINK It's all right.

WAITER (*Holding his hand out.*) Five pounds twenty.

Link pays the money. Waiter hands the order over.

GINGER Thanks Link.

LINK Filled all the forms in at the DSS last week. They want me to go back in a couple of days.

GINGER Did you tell them you were a dosser?

LINK Yeah. They've just got to make their minds up about how I got here. It's OK Ginger, this'll last me till they come up with something.

GINGER (*Under his breath.*) You'll be lucky.

Lights fade down then up again as Ginger and Link are leaving the kebab house. They wrap themselves up. Ginger puts his hat on.

LINK Is this Oxford Street?

GINGER It doesn't matter mate, just keep moving. Cold'll get to you otherwise.

People going to work start to enter. Ginger eyes up the passers-by and straightens his clothes.

LINK What are you doing?

GINGER Watch this, me old son, you're about to get your first survival lesson. Watch the master at work.

Ginger walks towards a Passer-by.

Got any spare change please mate?

Passer-by ignores him and walks on. Ginger spots his

next target. As he walks towards him, three people enter and form a bus queue.

GINGER   Ten pence for a cup of tea mate?

*No response. **Ginger** steps in front of him, he still doesn't stop.*

Go on mate, just 10p, that's all.

*Exit **Passer-by**. **Ginger** gives him the 'V' sign. **Ginger** and **Link** laugh to each other. **Ginger** spots the bus queue. He takes out a sign with '14 and homeless' written on it, along with a battered McDonald's cup. He puts some change in it and approaches people in the queue.*

BUS QUEUER 1   *(Shaking their head.)* Don't carry cash, sorry.

GINGER   How you going to pay for the bus then?

BUS QUEUER 1   *(Patting his pocket.)* Bus pass.

BUS QUEUER 2   *(Lowers newspaper.)* Get lost. Go on, piss off!

*Ginger walks back to **Link**.*

LINK   How much did you get then, mighty Lord and Master?

GINGER   Not a bloody sausage. Miserable herberts these lot. You'll get so you can spot them a mile off.

LINK   Who?

GINGER   Them who won't give you anything. I'll show you, look. This is your expressionless moron who just looks through yer and walks past. *(**Ginger** does the act as **Link** tries to tap from him.)* Then there's your Mr Angry. Stuck so far up, he can't see the light of day. *(Play at tapping.)* 'Get lost, sod off!' And you've got your head shakers. *(Shakes his head furiously.)* Really get up my nose, them. I tell yer, one of these days, their heads'll come right off.

LINK   That all of them then?

GINGER   No, there's the worst of the lot. The pious,
         pathetic... pocket-patters.

         *The lads approach each other. **Ginger** starts to pat his
         pocket, getting faster the closer they get to one
         another; it ends up like a drum roll. **Ginger** takes a
         bow. They laugh, then sit down.*

LINK   So how do you spot the ones who will give you
         something?

GINGER   Instinct.

         *Enter **Shelter**, preoccupied.*

LINK   Yeah, but what would they look like?

GINGER   Sad, you know. Your do-gooder type, bit
         churchified. The sort that help the likes of us cos it
         makes them feel better.

LINK   (*Pointing at **Shelter**.*) Like him over there?

         ***Ginger** spots him and runs over, blocking his path.
         Shelter wakes from his daydream.*

GINGER   Sorry mate, you haven't got 20p to spare have yer?

         ***Shelter** just looks him up and down.*

         Go on mister. (*Pleading.*) Bit of change, that's all.
         Haven't had a hot meal all week.

SHELTER Change? (*Standing tall, eye to eye.*) I'd give you
         change my lad, ...if I had you in khaki for six
         weeks.

         ***Shelter** pushes **Ginger** aside and marches away from
         them. **Link** and **Ginger** start laughing. **Shelter**
         watches from a distance. Blackout.*

SCENE 15

*Shelter's room. **Shelter** holds a photo in one hand
and a clump of tatty-looking hair in the other. The
camera and tin are on the table and the trap door is
open.*

SHELTER (*Recording.*) Finished preparing number three.
(*Holding hair out.*) Can't have them joining the
ranks with rat tails. (*Sticking the photo to the back of
the picture.*) Fed Sappho while he had his bath, then
sent him away... with the sharp edge of a Kit-e-kat
tin. Took three hours to clean the blood up but...
(*Do-gooder voice.*) heck, it was worth it. (*Picks up
the clump of hair again, puts it in the tin.*) Have
identified two others. (*Puts the tin under the floor.*)
Filthy scum bags had the audacity to laugh at me.
(*Laughs himself as he puts the camera under the
floor.*) Well, nothing wrong in having a laugh, is
there Sappho? Next time I see either of those two,
I'll have them in stitches!

*Slams the trap door shut. Lights cross-fade to street.
Camden market. A number of **shoppers** enter and
mill around, making the place look busy. Enter **Link**
and **Ginger**.*

GINGER Feel better for that.

LINK It was embarrassing. You see the way that fella
looked at us?

GINGER So what? No laws against having a wash is there?

LINK No, but there's probably some about washing your
skiddy undies in a public lav.

GINGER They shouldn't have been staring.

LINK You were totally starkers, what did you expect?

GINGER What's the matter with you? You've been like this
all bloody morning.

LINK   Had some bad news that's all. I think the time has come for me to make some dosh.

Ginger looks at him in surprise.

Camden market, here I come!

Ginger smiles and watches **Link** *pacing up and down.* **Link** *approaches the punters.*

Spare any change love?

WOMAN   Get out of my way.

LINK   Have a nice day missus. (*To another.*) Spare any change mate?

MAN   Go on, get lost, piss off!

Man exits briskly, muttering under his breath. **Link** *sits down, next to* **Ginger**.

GINGER   Can't win 'em all.

Link's face is picked out in a spot. At the other side of the stage, **Trina** *appears. A benefit officer, she is sitting behind a window.* **Link** *is re-living the conversation they'd had earlier.*

TRINA   They've managed to make a decision Mr erm…

LINK   Hughes.

TRINA   That's right.

LINK   Does it say how much I'll be getting?

TRINA   Have a look shall we… (*Phone rings.*) Hello, benefit office, Trina speaking… Hold please. Thank you. (*To* **Link**.) Sorry about that. So, you applied for severe hardship entitlement on account of you being homeless at the moment, that right?

LINK   Yeah.

TRINA   Yes, let's see then… (*Reading a form.*) Aah, aha, mmm, ahaa.

LINK   How much is it then?

TRINA   Based on the information you supplied in your application, the adjudicating officer has deemed fit to see that you're not entitled I'm afraid.

LINK   But I haven't got anywhere to live.

TRINA   That's because you left home though isn't it.

LINK   But I did what anyone else would have done in my situation, I had no choice.

TRINA   But you made yourself homeless Mr Hughes. It's been decided.

LINK   Can I apply for something else.

TRINA   Yes...

LINK   I'll do that then.

TRINA   ...once you've turned eighteen. (*Gets back to her phone.*) Hello, still there?... Yeah.. Aha... Wrong department I'm afraid...

     *DSS scene fades. Lights back on **Link** and **Ginger**.*

GINGER   So, out with it!

LINK   Out with what?

GINGER   This bad news of yours.

LINK   (*Lying.*) Dog's died. Rang our Carol before.

GINGER   Oh, sorry mate...

LINK   Has it ever struck you how much money people waste on crap?

GINGER   All the time.

LINK   Look at that. She just handed over ten quid for a candle. (*Pointing.*) They'll refuse you ten pence for a cup of tea then think nothing of spending pounds on rubbish like that.

GINGER   They won't give you anything if you don't ask though.

*Link gets up and continues to beg from the passing shoppers. As he does this, **Toya** and **Greg** enter. She goes over to **Ginger**.*

GINGER   All right you two, how's it going?

TOYA   Same old stuff I suppose, how about you?

GINGER   Just had a good wash mate.

GREG   Wondered what the sweet smell was.

*They laugh. **Link** strolls over.*

LINK   (*Pretending to be hard.*) Now then, Link's the name. I'm... doing some begging with Ginger.

*They virtually ignore him. **Link** backs away.*

TOYA   Where did you find him?

GINGER   He's OK. (*Quietly.*) Bit soft that's all.

TOYA   I don't suppose you've seen Doggy Bag on your travels?

GINGER   He owe you money or something?

GREG   No. He's just gone.

LINK   Maybe he got a job or something.

TOYA   (*Sarcastically.*) And you'd know all about it, would you?

GINGER   Anyhow, I thought it'd be Nick you were looking for.

TOYA   Watch it you.

LINK   (*To **Greg**.*) What's he on about?

GREG   This lad she fancies.

TOYA   I don't fancy Nick, right, will you get that into your thick heads.

GINGER   Ah, the lady dosser doth protest a bit too much.
         What do you reckon Greg?

TOYA   Pack it in.

GINGER   Should have heard him the other day.
         (*Impersonating* **Nick**.) 'All right there Ginger man,
         how's it hanging? Seen Toya lately, I really dig that
         chick.'

LINK   Sounds like a right hippie.

TOYA   (*To* **Link**.) Met him then?

LINK   No.

TOYA   I'm going for a kip while the rain stays off. (*To*
         Greg.) Coming?

GREG   Yeah. See yer Ginge.

GINGER   See yer mate.

         Toya and *Greg* exit.

LINK   Who's this Doggy Bag then?

GINGER   Just some lad. Couldn't bring himself to beg, so he
         started hanging round cafes waiting for people to
         leave stuff.

LINK   He eats their left-overs?

GINGER   Yeah. Scoops them into a plastic bag and has his
         own little take-away, that's how he got his name.

LINK   Horrible isn't it?

GINGER   Hmm?

LINK   His mum and dad must have been really proud of
         him at some point.

GINGER   What?

LINK   I wonder what they called him.

GINGER   Bet yer it wasn't Doggy Bag.

LINK   Bet they'd never have guessed he'd end up out
        here either. Fancy going missing and not one
        person being bothered.

GINGER *(Realising **Link** is upset.)* It's best not to think about
        it Link. Honest.

LINK   If you say so.

GINGER Come on. I've got a surprise.

        *Lights fade as **Link** packs his things together. Both
        exit.*

SCENE 16

        *Camden Lock. The stage is dark with lights casting a
        blue, rippling effect. Sound of lapping water. **Hook** is
        sitting on a folding chair. He's wearing wellies, a wax
        jacket and appears to be asleep. Enter **Link** and
        Ginger.*

LINK   So, this is it. Another bit of the rat-infested canal.

GINGER Will you stop whinging.

LINK   Where's the big surprise then?

GINGER *(Pointing to **Hook**.)* See the fella with the wellies?

LINK   Yeah.

GINGER That's Captain Hook, our new landlord ...for
        tonight anyhow.

LINK   So, where's this gaff then?

GINGER See that old barge behind him?

LINK   *(Sees it.)* You... are... joking?

GINGER *(Moving towards **Hook**.)* Come on.

LINK   How much is it anyway?

GINGER Three quid a night. I'll sort it, someone coughed up
        a tenner they owed me.

LINK   Doesn't look very safe to me. How does he get away with it?

GINGER   It's for dossers remember. Come on.

Hook suddenly pipes up, making the lads jump.

HOOK   Weren't thinking about sneaking past were you lads?

GINGER   Wouldn't dream of it Hook. Any room at the inn?

HOOK   Yes. If you can pay for it.

GINGER   (*Handing money over.*) We'll take the presidential suite in that case.

HOOK   (*Snatching the cash.*) Hilarious.

GINGER   And would you take our bags up my good man?

HOOK   Lad crushed his leg last night. Slipped as he was climbing aboard. Mind you don't do the same.

GINGER   Thanks for the warning.

HOOK   Made hell of a mess of the paintwork.

Hook laughs.

LINK   (*To **Ginger**.*) Scratched a bit of rust off more like.

HOOK   There's no rust on that beauty. You're looking at five star accommodation there.

GINGER   Don't see you kipping on it do we Hook?

HOOK   No son. Don't like depriving the likes of you that's why. Be sure to call room service if you need anything.

GINGER   (*Moving away from **Hook**.*) Right you are your worship.

LINK   Thinks he's a right comedian doesn't he?

GINGER   He's all right, Hook. Nowhere near as hard as he pretends to be.

LINK   This looks spooky.

GINGER Might not be a hotel in the Caribbean, Link, but it beats the hell out of kipping in doorways, especially in this weather.

LINK   What if it sinks?

GINGER Won't sink mate. It'll stink a bit though. Come on.

Lights dim. Sound changes to creaking, snoring and dripping.

LINK   (*Peering into the darkness.*) Phwarrr! This must be the most disgusting place on earth. Smells like a cow-shed. (*Sniffs and coughs.*) Smells worse than a cow-shed. (*Steps on someone.*)

DOSSER Eh, watch it!

LINK   There must be a hundreds of 'em. Hundreds of stinking, sweaty bodies.

GINGER (*Pointing to an area of floor.*) There's a couple of spaces there.

They squeeze into a gap on the floor.

        Sweet dreams.

LINK   Yeah, sure.

Link lies down. Echoes of Ginger saying the word 'Caribbean' fade in with heavenly music, soft and dreamlike. A chorus of dossers get up, shed their blankets and become the characters from previous scenes.

VINCE   Here he his, Stig of the Dump!

JOAN   Vince, don't.

VINCE   (*Threatening.*) Don't what?

CAROL   (*Pointing to an empty space.*) This is your chair Dave.

VINCE   Yeah, the one covered in plastic.

Link tosses and turns.

LANDLORD Listen sunshine, it's me who makes the rules round here and today's rule is, you either pay up or you get out!

LINK You'll get your money, I'm getting my first wages Monday morning. I told the boss I'd need 'em so I could pay you.

LINK (*In his sleep.*) I'll get you for this! (*Pause.*) I just wanted...

ATTENDANT We all 'just want' a lot of things, but most of us believe in paying for them first.

TRINA Based on the information you supplied in your application, the adjudicating officer has deemed fit to see that you're not entitled I'm afraid. Sorry.

LINK But I haven't got anywhere to live.

TRINA That's because you left home though isn't it.

GINGER (*Off.*) It might not be a hotel in the Caribbean... Caribbean... Caribbean...

*Up-tempo, tropical music comes in, e.g. Kokomo, the Beach Boys. Lights become bright and colourful. This time, the **dossers** become servants lavishing **Link** and **Ginger** with extravagant gifts and food. An Hawaiian dancer appears in front of **Link**. He gets up and starts to join in. Lights snap back and the music stops. **Dossers** shout and moan at **Link** for dancing on them. **Link** lies down again. There is a pause, then a loud, resonant fart is heard. **Ginger** wakes up.*

GINGER (*To **Link**.*) Was that you?

LINK Shut up, no.

Lights fade to black.

END OF ACT ONE

ACT TWO

Scene 1

> *The Daily Tribune office. **Louise** takes a scruffy-looking jumper from an Oxfam bag and tries it against herself for size. **Gavin** appears behind her.*

Gavin Louise?

Louise What now?

Gavin Relax. I'm not going to give you a hard time, OK? Just wanted you to have this. (*Hands her a mobile phone.*) In case of emergencies.

Louise How many homeless kids have you seen with these Gavin?

Gavin I don't know. The ones with wealthy parents might have them.

Louise Haven't you got a story to cover?

Gavin Come home in the evenings. You don't have to stay out there all night.

Louise No.

Gavin I'll meet you then. I'll get hold of some scruffy clothes and bring you a sandwich.

> *Pause*

Louise I'll call you. (*Gives him a peck on the cheek then exits.*)

SCENE 2

> *Shelter's* room. ***Shelter*** *is recording.*

SHELTER Spotted my laughing boys today. This morning it was, laying about with some other low-lifes in Camden Lock.

> *Spot comes up on **Link** and **Ginger** laughing in the street.*

Oh yes, knew it was them. Wouldn't forget a couple of disgusting scruffs like that in a hurry. Managed to discover their names too… Link and Ginger.

> *Light goes down on **Link** and **Ginger**.*

I shall study them. Get to know the target. Know where they go. Know what they do. Know what you think, Link.

> *Light comes up again on the street. This time, we see a group of eight **dossers**.*

Stick together, mostly. Safety in numbers.

> *Two of the **dossers** exit.*

Just need to bide my time, keep an eye on things. Everything comes to those who wait.

> *Three others leave together.*

And I'm waiting for the laughing boys. Waiting for one of them to be a-l-l alone.

> *Remaining two **dossers** leave, to reveal **Link** and **Ginger** sleeping behind them.*

And whichever one I get first, gets this!

> ***Shelter*** *picks up a hammer. His room snaps to black.*

SCENE 3

*The street. **Link** in a doorway. He looks scruffier now. His sleeping bag has lost its bright, Christmassy look.*

NICK   (Off.) Big Issue.

Link wakes suddenly as though waking from a bad dream.

LINK   Ginger!

NICK   (*Entering.*) Big Issue. Help the homeless.

LINK   Some of us were trying to kip.

NICK   Sorry man.

LINK   Man? (*Goes over to **Nick**.*) You wouldn't be Nick by any chance?

NICK   (*Showing his badge.*) The very same.

LINK   I'm a mate of Ginger's.

NICK   Right! (*Calling.*) Big Issue!

LINK   You're the one who fancies Toya aren't you?

NICK   Who told you that?

LINK   Ginger. You know, black coat, green bobble-hat...?

NICK   Sorted, yeah. Saw him couple of days ago.

LINK   You're joking. Tuesday night?

NICK   What's the big deal?

LINK   Where was he?

NICK   Just there. Came out of the station and started talking to some old dude.

LINK   I was supposed to meet him but I fell asleep. Haven't seen him since.

NICK   (*Calls.*) Help the homeless! (*To **Link**.*) Yeah. Pretty heavy scene man. Him and the old geezer were giving it rock all. Something about an accident and hospital. I could hear them. They went off somewhere then.

LINK   Together?

NICK   Yeah.

LINK   If you see him again, will you tell him Link's been looking for him?

NICK   That you?

LINK   Yeah.

NICK   Feeling better then?

LINK   Sorry?

NICK   Old geezer said it was you who'd had the accident. (*Running it through in his head with a bad impersonation of **Shelter**.*) 'Ruddy darn mess he's in... poor little... Link!' (*As himself again.*) Yup, definitely said Link. And he was sort of 'off it', you know, pulling the Ginger lad along with him.

*Enter **Toya** wearing same coat as **Ginger**, with the hood up.*

LINK   Did you see where they went?

NICK   It's my job to sell these mate. (*Lifting magazines.*) I'm not the F.B.I.

***Link** spots **Toya** and mistakes her for **Ginger**.*

LINK   Thanks Nick.

NICK   No sweat.

LINK   I don't believe it! (*Runs over to **Toya**.*) Ginger! I've been worried sick... (***Toya** takes the hood off. **Link** sees that it's not **Ginger**.*) ...Sorry, I thought...

TOYA   Don't worry about it.

LINK   (*Realising who she is.*) You're the girl from the market, right? (*Introducing himself.*) Link. I was with

56

Ginger?

TOYA Lost him have you?

LINK (*Disappointed.*) I was hoping you'd tell me. Did he meet you and Greg on Tuesday night?

TOYA Yeah, left about tennish to get back to you. Will you do us a favour?

Nick spots Toya and slowly makes his way over. She can't see him.

LINK S'pose.

TOYA (*Takes a note from her pocket.*) Will you give this to the Big Issue lad for me?

LINK Yeah.

TOYA Wait till I've gone though, and don't read it, right?

LINK Anything else your ladyship?

Nick sneaks up.

NICK Toya!

TOYA (*Stuffs note back into her pocket then pretends to be surprised.*) All right?

NICK Did you come to see me?

TOYA Erm... no, not especially.

LINK Do you know of any old fellas Ginger was friendly with round here?

TOYA There's Hook I suppose. Why?

LINK Would Hook hang around the station?

TOYA Shouldn't think so, he only lives round the corner.

NICK (*To Toya.*) Do you want a Big Issue? You can have it for free?

TOYA Why don't you give it to Link.

LINK He's gone missing. If you see him...

57

TOYA   I'll tell him to look you up.

LINK   Thanks. (*To Toya.*) Good luck.

      Exit Link.

NICK   What was that about?

TOYA   Nothing.

      Exit Toya embarrassed. Lights fade to black.

SCENE 4

      A cafe. Cafe-owner. Louise (now in the persona of Gail) is sitting on her own at a table. She is wearing the scruffy jumper but still looks clean and fresh. When she speaks it is with a slight Scottish accent. Enter Link. He spots her straight away and stands there staring. She finishes the tea she's drinking then goes straight to the counter. Link sits in her chair.

GAIL   (*To cafe-owner*) Can of coke please.

OWNER   You've got a thirst 'ant yer?

      Gail smiles.

      Sixty-five please love.

      She hands him the money, takes the can and goes back to her table. Link jumps up and knocks her. She touches his arm.

GAIL   I'm sorry!

LINK   (*Delirious.*) I'm not! I mean, erm... forget it.

      Gail lets out a little laugh and sits down. Link goes to the counter.

      Tea please. (*Hands him the money.*) Small one.

      Link tries to sneak glances without her noticing. She catches him out and laughs.

OWNER   (*Handing a small cup over.*) Eh, Romeo!

LINK   What? (*Coming round.*) Oh, thanks. (*He takes the cup and looks round for somewhere to sit.*)

GAIL   Sit here if you like.

Link puts his fist up and, without Gail seeing, mimes an enthusiastic 'Yes!' He sits next to her and takes a sip of tea.

GAIL   Been in London long?

Link is in such a hurry to answer he forgets to swallow the tea.

LINK   Oh, ages.

It pours from his mouth. He wipes the mess up with his sleeve and tries to pretend it hasn't happened. Gail tries not to laugh.

Years, I've been here years, yeah.

GAIL   You know your way around then?

LINK   (*Shrugs, trying to be cool.*) S'pose.

GAIL   So, what do they call you?

LINK   Link.

GAIL   Link. (*Takes a sip of coke.*)

LINK   It's short for something. I, er, don't tell people my real name. Low profile and that, yer know?

GAIL   That's fine. (*Holding her hand out.*) I'm Gail.

Link and Gail shake hands. Link holds on just a little too long.

LINK   Just got here, right?

GAIL   Right.

LINK   Where from? Sorry, you don't have to tell me if you don't want.

GAIL   Glasgow.

LINK   Heavy scene?

GAIL   Aye, stepfather.

LINK   Same here! (*Cool again.*) Had to get out in the end, the man was an animal.

GAIL   Mine too. I tell yer, it should be them out here, not us.

LINK   Or we should have them put in a zoo.

They laugh.

LINK   (*He drains his mug and gets up. Back to* **Gail***.*) I'd better get going.

GAIL   Why?

LINK   Things to do.

Link starts to exit. Gail stops him.

GAIL   Don't go. (*Pause.*) I'm scared, Link. Feels like I haven't spoken to anyone in days.

LINK   (*Sitting down again. He sounds like an expert.*) We're all scared Gail, you get used to it. In fact it's probably being scared that keeps us alive.

GAIL   Listen, I know this is going to sound cheeky but I'm new to all this and you really seem to know what you're doing. (*Pause.*) Can I hang around with you? Just for a couple of days? I've got money! (*Corrects herself.*) ...left, erm, a bit anyway.

Link is just staring, ecstatic at the suggestion.

It's OK. I'm sorry, really I am. (*Gets up herself.*) I'd better leave you in peace.

LINK   (*Waking up.*) Where are you going?

Gail turns. They look at each other for an instant, then smile. Gail sits down again. The Caribbean Paradise music from the end of Act One drifts in as lights cross-fade to **Shelter's** *room.* **Shelter** *in his*

chair with Sappho on his lap. He is surrounded by
army boots. The biscuit tin is on the table. He holds
the cat in a gentle embrace and talks to it.

SHELTER Oh, Sappho. Link the stink's in love, and laughing
boy two's up shit creek. (*He kneels, carefully places*
the cat on the floor beside him, then picks up a pair
of boots.) They're not mine, boy. These are for our
little army. Bit on the large side most of them… But
not going to be marching very far though, are they?
(*Has a little laugh to himself. Gets up, goes over to*
the fireplace and turns the picture over.) Beautiful!
And to think not long ago they were all nothing
short of scum. (*Opens the biscuit tin.*) Let's have a
look at daddy's trophies shall we Sappho?

He takes a watch, gold chain, belt-buckle and clump
of hair from the tin. He starts to shine the buckle with
the hair almost affectionately.

Four new friends to play with now. Four smart,
obedient soldiers. The Camden Horizontals. Room
in the barracks for a few more yet mind.

Switches his radio on. Another military, marching tune
is heard. **Shelter** *opens his trap door and pulls out*
four pairs of tatty, blood-stained trainers. He throws
them onto the fire and starts to put his souvenirs
back into the tin, accidentally knocking the watch
under the table. He does not notice this. He goes
back to his chair, picks up his dictaphone and starts
recording.

Target finally on its own today, though sadly, was
intercepted by tatty-looking female. Not to worry,
everything comes to those who wait. (*Stops*
recording.) No rest for the wicked!

Goes back to the trap door. He pulls a pair of legs
from the hole. They are wearing army trousers.
Shelter *starts to put a pair of boots onto the body.*
Lights and music fade out.

SCENE 5

> *A public lavatory.* **Link** *is singing to himself while having a wash. He feels like a man of the world, scrutinising himself in a mirror. A* **Businessman** *walks in and looks frightened. Enter* **Greg**.

GREG   Vandalism now is it?

> *Link turns round but doesn't recognise him.*

GREG   If your voice doesn't shatter it, your face will. Greg.

LINK   Oh, yeah. Sorry.

GREG   Hear your mate Ginger did a runner with Hook.

LINK   Wasn't Hook. I went to his flat and asked him about it.

GREG   Didn't he tell you to do one?

LINK   Nah, he was all right really. He was outside, knocking for the fella underneath him. Said he was worried cos he hadn't seen him for a bit.

GREG   What about Ginger?

LINK   No.

GREG   He'll be around somewhere.

LINK   Can I ask you something, Greg?

GREG   Sure.

LINK   Have you had a girlfriend since you've become a dosser?

GREG   Looking like this? What do you want to know that for?

LINK   No reason.

GREG   No reason for all this washing yourself and singing at the top of your voice either then? Come on, out with it.

LINK Met her yesterday. Should've seen the way she was looking at me. I tell you mate, if I have that effect on women in this state, can't imagine what I could do scrubbed up.

Link scrubs under his arms then stops and becomes pensive.

BUSINESSMAN (*Exiting.*) You are a disgrace!

LINK You're not such a pretty sight yourself mate.

Link and Greg laugh. Greg starts to wash also.

Have you ever had a girlfriend?

GREG There was someone back home, yeah.

LINK Changes the way you look at things doesn't it.

GREG Suppose. This your first?

LINK No. I had loads before I started dossing. Gail she's called. Nice name isn't it.

GREG Got any soap I can borrow.

*Link hands him a bar of soap. Enter **Nick**.*

LINK Gail. Gail, Gail, Gail...

NICK Help the homeless!

GREG You won't sell many of them in here mate.

NICK Force of habit. (*Goes to pee.*) So what's new?

GREG Link's got a girlfriend.

NICK Link?

LINK (*Acting casual.*) Yeah. You managed to get off with Toya yet?

NICK Joking aren't you. She won't give me the time of day.

*Enter **Businessman 2**. He also looks frightened.*

LINK She's probably shy. You should just go up and ask

her like I did with Gail.

GREG Where is this Gail then?

LINK Gone to call her sister in Glasgow. (*Takes his trainers off and starts to scrub his feet.*) Put her mind at rest you know, now she's found someone to protect her.

GREG How you gonna do that?

NICK Show his feet off.

Man enters and starts to wash his hands. He gives Link a dirty look.

LINK Funny. I am getting used to all this now. There was a time I wouldn't be seen dead doing this sort of thing.

Starts to take his pants off. Man and Businessman 2 are visibly shocked.

NICK Take a look at the Big Issue, gents?

The lads laugh as the men leave the toilet in shock. Lights fade to black.

SCENE 6

Shelter's room. Enter Shelter, marching. Sappho is curled up on the chair. Shelter salutes him.

SHELTER (*Recording.*) Been very busy since the last entry. Recruited another three, which makes seven in total. Seven less bone-idle work-shies for the nation to worry about. Idiot upstairs offered the use of his video. Decided to take him up on it. As he goes out for some of the evening to tend his floating dosshouse, I was left with an opportunity. Arrived before he left of course. Dirtied a mug or two, put cassette in the machine, then made sure I was back asleep in front of the TV for when he returned. I deserve a medal. (*Puts the dictaphone down and snatches a piece of paper.*) Aww, listen to this, Sappho. (*Reads.*) 'Dear Nick, I've fancied you for ages...' (*Laughs.*) Poor fella. (*Continues to read.*) '...wanted to mention it but there always seems to be someone around...' Well, there would be on a street, wouldn't there, number seven. It's what streets are for – moving along, not dossing down on. (*Throws the paper on the fire.*) Not to worry, got a roof over your head now girl, and a floor. (*Laughs. Then, exiting marching.*) Camden Horizontals, fall in!

*Lights cross-fade to reveal **Gail/Louise** in a public phone booth. She is trying to make herself heard above the thudding beat emanating from a nearby nightclub. We see people entering and leaving under the **Bouncer's** watchful eye.*

LOUISE   (*On the phone.*) Nothing positive Sir, just an older man, that's all I've managed to... It's only been a couple of... Yes Mr Stamp, as soon as anything out of the ordinary happens... Can you pass a message on to Gavin for me?

*She spots **Link** approaching. Puts on her Scottish accent.*

Doesn't matter, have to go. See you Jane.

Puts receiver down.

LINK   Guess who?

GAIL   You were quick.

LINK   Sister OK then?

GAIL   How did the job hunting go this afternoon? I forgot to ask.

LINK   No joy. I did try, they just weren't having any.

GAIL   That's OK.

LINK   I just wish I could look after you, treat you like a proper girlfriend.

GAIL   I don't expect it Link. You're just right as you are.

LINK   A dosser. Yeah, I can believe that. I'm gonna try to get us into a hostel. Easier to find work once you've got an address. It'll be OK Gail, I promise.

GAIL   You're a nice lad Link.

LINK   Lad? You sound like my mum.

Link tries to put his arm around Gail. She subtly backs away.

GAIL   We should be in a place like that right now.

A clubber is thrown out by the Bouncer. Link and Gail laugh. Enter Middle-aged man. He's studying a street map of London. He looks anxious. He approaches Link and Gail.

MAN   I wonder if you could help me? I'm trying to trace my daughter, and I wondered if you might have seen her? (*Takes a photo from his shoulder bag, then passes it to them.*) Her name's Tanya.

GAIL   (*Shaking her head.*) Sorry, can't say that I have. Link?

Gail hands Link the photo. He has his back to the man. He takes a glance, then speaks without even turning.

LINK   (*Nonchalant.*) Yeah, once or twice.

Link passes the photo back, over his shoulder. The Man takes the photo with one hand and pulls Link around with the other.

MAN   Have you spoken to her, did she say where she was living?

LINK   (*Half-laughing.*) Living? She was a dosser mate, like us.

Man is visibly upset.

She sometimes hung around the market if it's any help.

MAN   When was the last time you saw her?

LINK   Don't know.

MAN   Was she with anyone, an older man perhaps?

LINK   (*Trying to impress* ***Gail***.) I'm a dosser mate, not the F.B.I.

MAN   (*Close to tears.*) Someone thought he'd seen Tanya talking to a neighbour of his. He spotted them by the tube station on his way home.

LINK   Tanya? She was called Toya mate, not...

GAIL   (*Nudging* ***Link***.) Were you christened 'Link'? (*To* ***Man***.) Who gave you that information?

MAN   A gentleman by the canal. He rents a barge.

LINK   Hook. What would Toya, 'Tanya', be hanging around Hook's neighbours for? He must have been having you on.

MAN   (*Handing the address to* ***Gail***.) I've called three times today, no one answered the door.

GAIL   Have you been to the police?

MAN   They said they'd look into it.

LINK   Won't break their necks, not if they knew she was a dosser.

MAN   (*Fighting back the tears.*) She's only seventeen. It's taken nearly six months to trace her to this area.

GAIL   I'm sure you'll find her soon enough. She can't be far away.

LINK   We'll look out for her.

GAIL   I'll give you my... (*Stops herself.*) ...give me your number. I'll call you if we hear anything.

Man writes on the paper.

MAN   Bless you.

*Takes a ten pound note out and presses it into **Link's** hand.*

Bless you both.

LINK   Thanks!

*Exit **Man**. Music from club gets louder.*

LINK   Come on.

***Link** leads **Gail** to the club. The **Bouncer** looks them up and down.*

BOUNCER   Go on! Get lost! Piss off!

The door slams in their faces. The music stops abruptly and the lights snap to black.

SCENE 7

*Camden market. **Link** is tapping. Recorded sound of phone ringing followed by the voices off of **Gail**/**Louise** calling her report through to **Gavin** at the office.*

GAVIN   *(Off.)* Daily Tribune?

LOUISE   *(Off.)* Gavin, it's me.

GAVIN   *(Off.)* Lou...

LOUISE   *(Off.)* Listen I don't have much time, get this down would you.

GAVIN   *(Off.)* One second... OK, shoot.

LOUISE   *(Off.)* Headline to read, 'Down and out – right dangerous'

GAVIN   *(Off.)* Go on.

LOUISE   *(Off.)* 'Tension mounts among the young and homeless as several of their number disappear. Our street level reporter is tracing the steps of the sinister street cleaner known as the...' What was the name he gave?

GAVIN   (*Off.*) Shelter, I think.

LOUISE   (*Off.*) '…known as "The Shelter". The only lead to
date is a possible eye-witness account describing
an older man. It is our understanding…'
(***Louise/Gail's*** *voice fades.*)

*Enter **Nick**.*

NICK   Yo, Link!

LINK   Hi Nick.

NICK   There's been some weird stuff happening round
here man, I tell yer. (*Shouts.*) Big Issue! This
morning right, some old geezer comes asking me
about his daughter, yeah…

LINK   Go on.

NICK   Harassed or what! Sad little bag on his shoulder,
know the type? Anyhow, only turns out to be Toya's
dad!

LINK   I've seen him. Spoke to me and Gail last night.

NICK   (*Takes the photo from his pocket.*) Gave me this. She
looks great cleaned up man.

LINK   Nick, when was the last time you saw her?

NICK   Couple of days ago now. Do you think she's all
right?

LINK   Her dad said she'd been seen knocking about with
some old guy.

NICK   Dod–gy or what? Could be the geezer I saw Ginger
with.

LINK   That's what I'm thinking. Maybe I should go to the
police.

NICK   Fuzz don't listen to dossers Link. Can't you find out
where the old guy lives?

LINK   I think I know.

NICK   Get round there man!

*Enter **Gail**.*

Want me to come with?

LINK   No, it's OK. We'll go.

GAIL   What's happening?

LINK   Need to check something out. See you later Nick.

NICK   No sweat Link.

***Link** and **Gail** start to exit.*

LINK   That sister must get sick of hearing from you...

*Exit **Link**. Lights fade on **Nick** as he looks at his photo.*

SCENE 8

***Shelter's** room. **Shelter** stands there with two **police officers** (**1**: female; **2**: male). He has his head down, looking at a photograph, though on first sight he appears to be hanging his head in shame.*

POLICE 1   Do you recognise the girl in the picture Sir?

SHELTER   I'm afraid not, officers. (*Hands the photograph back.*)

POLICE 1   Is it true that you entertain younger people here?

SHELTER   I wouldn't call it that...

POLICE 2   Answer the question please Sir.

SHELTER   There have been a couple of the youngsters here, but...

POLICE 1   Look at the picture again. Has this person been on your property Sir?

SHELTER   No. I told you I haven't seen this one before.

POLICE 2   We have it on good authority that you have been in contact with this girl.

SHELTER On occasion, I will talk to them and yes, even invite one into my home. One dosser looks pretty much the same as another officer. But I assure you, I haven't seen her before. Whoever told you otherwise must have been mistaken.

POLICE 1 Do they usually spend the night with you Sir?

SHELTER Certainly not.

POLICE 1 You realise how dangerous it is opening your home up to these people, do you sir?

SHELTER I do now. (*Rolls up his sleeves to show deep scratches.*) This is the thanks I got.

POLICE 2 What did you expect?

SHELTER Will that be all officers?

POLICE 1 Not quite. Can you tell us where you were on the night of the fourth?

SHELTER This month?

POLICE 1 Yes, this month.

SHELTER Fourth, would that be Tuesday last? Ah, yes, I can tell you that. I was with the gentleman upstairs. We watch the occasional video, have a couple of drinks now and then. Nice chap. I'm sure he'd be able to confirm...

POLICE 1 (*Looking through her note book. She nods at her colleague.*) Thank you for your time Sir. We may however need to speak to you again.

SHELTER Of course. I hope you find what you are looking for.

POLICE 2 We'll see ourselves out.

SHELTER As you please.

Exit **Police**. **Shelter** *waits for the sound of the door.*

SHELTER Magnificent. Absolutely, bloody magnificent.

SCENE 9

*Outside **Shelter's** flat. **Link** and **Gail** are crouched behind a couple of dustbins.*

LINK Don't think anything's going to happen here. How long has it been now?

GAIL Show some patience Link.

LINK It could be any of these houses. The fella said he was a neighbour, it doesn't have to be the bloke that lives underneath him does it.

***Shelter** comes out of his front door.*

GAIL Shhh!

LINK (*Whisper.*) Doesn't look much like an abductor to me.

GAIL He's hardly gonna have it tattooed to his forehead is he. Shush. He's coming over.

***Link** and **Gail** get lower as **Shelter** walks past them, whistling 'Morning has broken'.*

Where do you think he's going?

LINK Church by the sound of it.

GAIL Maybe we should follow him.

LINK We've been waiting nearly two hours to see a nice little man go for a morning stroll. We're a couple of dossers, not Mulder and Scully.

GAIL I don't like it.

LINK How many other people spend their Sunday mornings crouched behind dustbins?

GAIL You're the one that wanted to come here. (*Pause.*) Breakfast in bed. That's how a Sunday should start.

LINK Yeah, so long as you don't spill it on the cardboard.

*They laugh. Pause. Enter **Shelter** carrying a*

newspaper and tin of cat food. This time he's singing 'Onward, Christian soldiers'.

GAIL   Get down!

They duck behind the bins. **Shelter** *goes back into his flat.*

That was close.

LINK   Yeah, we nearly got hymned to death. Do you honestly think that's him?

GAIL   He was seen talking to them.

LINK   Talking to someone's not a criminal offence though. Look at him, he's a 'do gooder', you can spot em a mile off.

GAIL   Oh no, I don't believe it! I've left my address book in the phone booth. I'll have to go and get it Link, it's got...

LINK   '...Jane's number in it', by any chance?

GAIL   I shouldn't be long. Keep your eyes peeled and be careful.

Exit **Gail**.

LINK   What does she want with an address book? She must know that number off by heart by now.

Door opens. **Shelter** *comes out in his slippers carrying a fork and a bowl of cat food.* **Link** *ducks.* **Shelter** *puts on the do-gooder bit, in case there are people around.*

SHELTER   Sappho! Come on boy, breakfast! It's your favourite, prawn and broccoli, big fella.

Link inches forward to get a better view, then knocks a dustbin lid off. **Shelter** *comes over.* **Link** *jumps up.*

LINK   I'm sorry mate, I was just... looking for something. (*Spots a crisp packet and grabs it.*) My crisps! I dropped them by accident and I was just picking them up.

SHELTER (*Softest voice imaginable.*) That's OK son, it's a free country. You haven't seen a little white cat around have you?

LINK (*Relaxing.*) No, sorry.

SHELTER He never used to be like this. Must've got himself a lady friend or something.

*Link glances in the direction **Gail** left in.*

LINK Yeah. (*Smiles, then pretends to eat a crisp for something to do.*)

SHELTER Sappho! (*To **Link**.*) Not many crisps left in that packet of yours.

LINK I like the salt in the bottom.

SHELTER (*Gentle.*) Want to tell me what you were really doing?

LINK I wasn't doing anything, I just...

SHELTER Came to see Mr Hook possibly?

LINK Yeah.

SHELTER Why didn't you say. He often has, erm, his residents calling.

LINK Is he in?

SHELTER Popped to the supermarket.

LINK Better go then.

SHELTER He won't be long. I asked him to get me some soup. Should've gone myself really but he did offer. (*Calls.*) Sappho! I presume you are one of his erm, boarders?

LINK When I can afford it.

SHELTER He'll come back when he's hungry enough. You're welcome to come in and wait for Mr Hook if you want.

LINK   (*Uncertain. He looks around for* **Gail**. *Perhaps he can impress her.*) You sure?

SHELTER   Yes. In fact, I've got an old coat in there all wrapped up and ready to take to the charity shop. You'd be saving me the trip if you took it off my hands.

LINK   I've already got one thanks.

SHELTER   One of your friends might like it. It's very warm... Might even find another packet of crisps too while I'm at it. You know where to find me.

Shelter goes inside, leaving the door open.

*Light up on **Gail/Louise** in phone booth.*

LOUISE   ...Hello, yes I'm still here, have you found the officer in charge yet? ...I don't care what he said, I need to speak... But I believe it to be more than just a missing person case... All right, just give me his name... (*Writes name down.*) Thank you!

SCENE 10

Shelter's flat. He glances out of the window.

SHELTER   Mmm, not as soft as you look boy. So close and yet, so far away. (*Talks to portrait.*) Better luck next time, eh General? Don't want to push our luck do we?

*Shelter meticulously removes a speck of dust from the mantlepiece. **Link** appears in the doorway and clears his throat.*

Lights up on phone booth.

LOUISE   ...But they might listen to you Sir... Report a disturbance then. And send a photographer... I'm sorry... Yes, yes I know you're the one who gives the orders... Oh just shut up and listen to me will you, take this name...

Light snaps off.

SHELTER	Come in young man. No need to be shy.
LINK	Feels weird.
SHELTER	How do you mean?
LINK	Haven't been inside someone's house for ages.
SHELTER	It's nothing fancy but I call it home. I'm sorry, I didn't mean to be so tactless.
LINK	Getting some free crisps aren't I? ...And a new coat for my girlfriend.
SHELTER	Girlfriend eh?
LINK	Yeah. We're gonna have a place like this one day.
SHELTER	I think you'll end up in a much better place than this.
LINK	Sure!
SHELTER	Crisps! Back in a jiffy. Make yourself at home.
LINK	Thanks.

*Exit **Shelter**. **Link** looks around. He smiles as he remembers **Ginger** and hears a past conversation.*

LINK	(*Off.*) So how do you spot the ones who will give you something?
GINGER	(*Off.*) Instinct.
LINK	(*Off.*) Yeah, but what would they look like?
GINGER	(*Off.*) Sad, you know. Your do-gooder type, bit churchified. The sort that help the likes of us cos it makes them feel better.

*He's brought out of the memory by **Shelter**.*

SHELTER	(*Off.*) Cheese and onion?
LINK	Great, yeah.

*He goes over to the picture. He's about to touch it when **Shelter** shouts once more.*

SHELTER   (*Off.*) Why not take the weight off your feet?

LINK   (*To himself.*) Why not indeed.

*He sits in **Shelter's** chair, then spots something under the table. He stoops to find a watch.*

Can't be.

*Sees the inscription. Enter **Shelter**, noticing **Link's** discovery. He quietly closes the door behind himself.*

SHELTER   Found something?

***Link** tries to hide the watch.*

LINK   (*Getting up.*) I've just remembered, I'm supposed to be meeting someone...

SHELTER   You all right son?

LINK   Fine. Yeah. I just...

SHELTER   (*Pushing **Link** back into the chair and losing the do-gooder voice.*) Don't sound very fine to me. What have you got?

LINK   Nothing.

***Shelter** slowly approaches **Link**.*

SHELTER   I don't know, try to help a kid out and this is how the scruffy little scum-bag re-pays you.

LINK   (*Starting to panic.*) I wasn't trying to nick it...

SHELTER   Of course not.

LINK   It was mine!

SHELTER   Nice try. (*Snatches the watch.*) Given to me by a Liverpudlian friend, this was. (*Reads inscription.*) 'To Dave, the best son in the world.' See. If this was yours, it would say, 'To Link the stink', wouldn't it?

LINK   You know my name!

SHELTER   (*Calmly.*) Oh yes. Your friend told me. What was that one called...? (*Snaps his fingers.*)

LINK	Ginger!
SHELTER	(*Wide, menacing eyes.*) That's it. Blurted it out while I was… (*Pause, smiles.*) putting him out of his misery.
LINK	No!
SHELTER	(*Snigger.*) Funny. You know that's exactly what he said.

*Shelter lunges for **Link**, who darts out of the way and heads for the window. He tries to open it.*

Oh, yes. Everything comes to those who wait. (*Opens the trap door then heads for the window.*) Come on stinky boy, it's reunion time.

*Shelter grabs **Link**.*

LINK	Get away from me!

*Shelter carries **Link** towards the trap door. **Link** grabs the curtains and pulls them down. **Link** struggles free and runs to the door. It won't open.*

LINK	My girlfriend knows where I am. She'll be here soon.
SHELTER	More the merrier. Got to hand it to you. Made me wait for this laughing boy. But that's OK. It's all over now.

*Shelter lunges for **Link** and wrestles him onto the floor.*

How would you like to see your old mate Ginger?

LINK	Bastard!
SHELTER	Oh dear, I think we'll have to wash the dosser's mouth out.
LINK	Get off. I want to go home.
SHELTER	Too late for that. You're in the army now my boy.

*Shelter manoeuvres **Link** above the hole in the floor.*

Meet the gang.

*Shelter shoves **Link's** head under the floor. **Link** starts to scream.*

LINK   I'm gonna puke.

*Shelter lifts **Link** back like a rag doll, and punches him in the stomach. **Link** throws up into the hole in the floor. **Shelter** grabs him by the throat.*

SHELTER   Puke away, soldier! You're the one who's got to lie in it.

LINK   (*Weak.*) Let go, I'm passing out.

SHELTER   That's the general idea, stinky boy, this is your 'passing out' parade, ...get it?

*Shelter laughs as he tightens his grip around **Link's** throat. **Link** is losing consciousness. We hear the door being kicked. It suddenly breaks open. Enter **Hook**, closely followed by **Gail**. **Hook** grabs **Shelter**. **Link** gasps for breath.*

SHELTER   Little rat attacked me.

*Gail helps **Link** to his feet.*

LINK   Gail, get out! He's mad. We were right, it's him. Get out.

GAIL   Shh. It's OK, Link.

SHELTER   Come on old man, you gonna take the word of 'that' against mine? I'm an ex-serviceman.

HOOK   (*Holding onto **Shelter**.*) You're an abomination.

GAIL   Get him out of here, would you.

*Hook takes **Shelter** out of the room.*

HOOK   Come on!

GAIL   What were you playing at, Link? I told you to be careful. If that guy upstairs hadn't been in... It doesn't bear thinking about.

LINK	That's Hook. ...Said he'd gone to the shops for him. I thought it would be OK. He's got Ginger, Gail...

*Gail comforts **Link**. Sound of police sirens, cars stopping and doors slamming.*

He knew my name, Gail, he knew who I was. And he knows about you. You've got to... (*He stops in mid-flow. Something is beginning to dawn on him but he can't quite work it out yet. He looks quizzically at* **Gail**.)

GAIL I'm so sorry Link.

POLICE 1 (*Off.*) Over here Sarge.

SHELTER (*Off.*) Get your hands off, I'm a British citizen...

HOOK (*Off.*) Watch it lads, he's stronger than he looks.

POLICE 2 (*Off.*) This way...

SHELTER (*Off.*) I'm innocent. I'm acting on orders by Her Majesty the Queen.

POLICE 1 (*Off.*) So are we. Get a move on.

Gail goes to the window.

LINK Did you bring the law?

GAIL Sort of, yes, but I came straight back. When I saw the curtain come down I went for Hook. It's all I could think of.

LINK (*Sitting up and rubbing his neck.*) What did you tell them? Nick says the police don't listen to...

GAIL Link, there's something I have to tell you.

*Enter **Gavin**.*

GAVIN Louise darling, Stamp called the mobile. You. Are. A. Genius!

*He takes a picture of **Link** and **Gail**.*

GAIL	(*Reticent.*) Link, this is Gavin. (*To Gavin.*) This is the boy I told you about.
LINK	Boy?
GAVIN	(*Condescending.*) So, you're the brave street person eh? Heard a lot about you, fella.

*Gavin puts his hand out. **Link** looks at it.*

LINK	(*To **Gail**.*) So who are you then?
GAIL	My name's Louise. Louise Bain. I'm a journalist.
LINK	And you've been after this nutter for months, right?
LOUISE	Link...
LINK	But instead of going to the police, you just stood by? Watched him pick us off one by one until you had enough for a good story. Is that it? (*Pause.*) You didn't give a shit about me, did you?
GAVIN	Hey, steady on, Louise saved your life remember.
LINK	One more word from you and I'll stuff that camera up your...
LOUISE	You've got it wrong Link. We thought it was a hoax at first. I had no idea it was going to be this serious. We didn't have any evidence. You've got to believe me.
LINK	Try asking Ginger if he believes you. He's down there. (*To **Gavin**.*) Take some pictures if you like – you could sell them to his mum and dad.

Gail takes out a wad of bank notes.

LOUISE	Link, I want you to have this.

*She hands **Link** the cash.*

LINK	That make it all right will it?
GAVIN	Do you know how much you've got there?
LINK	(*He looks at the money.*) If I were a TV hero I'd

> throw this in your face. But TV heroes don't have to live on the street, right?
>
> *Gavin picks **Link's** pack up.*

LOUISE   Link, I'm so sorr…

LINK   Save it. You've got a big story to write, remember. Who knows, might even do some good if you get your facts straight. One or two of your cosy little readers might realise something. …(*To **Gavin**.*) That 'street persons' have got feelings, same as everyone else.

> ***Gavin** smiles apologetically then hands **Link** his pack. **Link** passes it to **Louise**.*

Something to remember me by. Louise!

> *Exit **Link**. **Gavin** tries to comfort **Gail**. She shrugs him off.*

SCENE 11

> ***Shelter** stands on one side of the stage. Excerpts of his recorded journal play back as he is very gradually lit from below.*

SHELTER   (*Off.*) …Prospect of a very prosperous winter…

…Didn't do anything dishonourable, of course. Just told her to get the soup down her neck, then gave it a little twist.

> *Lights fade up to reveal **Link** on the opposite side of the stage, as faint marching is heard.*

…Recruited another three which makes seven in total. Seven less bone-idle work-shies for the nation to worry about.

LINK   Justice was done, right?

> *The entire cast march slowly and silently in through the auditorium, dressed in the uniforms of the*

'Camden Horizontals', their faces chillingly pale and frozen.

'Shelter', that's what he called himself. Shelter got life. Now there's a thought, 'life'. Means he gets a roof, a bed, and three square meals a day. In the meantime I'm not sure what I'm going to do. I might try the Embankment or Covent Garden. There're a lot of us 'round Covent Garden. 'Course, I might leave London altogether.

What's your town like?

By the time he finishes the cast are marching silently on the stage. On a screen behind, a close up of **Link***. As the light dims on the real* **Link***, the slide changes to a longer shot showing him tapping in a busy street. Then a longer shot still – he is merging into the crowd.*

SHELTER   *(Smiling. Obsessed.)* T'ENTION!

The cast come to a sharp halt. The light on **Link** *has gone completely. The slide just shows a crowded street. Blackout.*

THE END

ACTIVITIES

THINGS TO TALK ABOUT

1 *I wonder what they called him.*

Bet yer it wasn't Doggy Bag.

Many of the characters in *Stone Cold* have 'assumed' names, but perhaps for different reasons. Talk about:

- why characters such as Gail, Link, Shelter and perhaps even Captain Hook don't use their real names;
- what the effect of never really finding out who the characters are might have on an audience.

2 Robert Swindells' novel is written in the 'first person'. That is, it is written as if Link is telling his own story. One result of this is that the reader does not discover that Gail is really a journalist until the very end, when Link himself realises the truth about her. In this play, the theatre audience know about Gail quite early on. Do you think that this spoils the effect or does it add something? Talk about how revealing Gail's true identity:

- might change the way an audience thinks and feels about her;
- could add to our understanding of Link;
- creates 'dramatic tension'. Look, for example, at Act Two Scene 6 (page 67), when Gail says to Tanya's father:
I'll give you my... (Stops herself.) ...give me your number. I'll call you if we hear anything.

3 The playwright, Joe Standerline, suggests that slides are used in the play. Look at Act One Scene 12 (page 34) and Act Two Scene 11 (page 83) and talk about:

- how these sequences could add to the dramatic effect of the play for an audience;

- where else slides might be used, and what they might show.

4 The concept of irony is quite difficult to explain, but an understanding of it is essential in making, performing and responding to drama. Sometimes irony is achieved by letting the audience know something that one of the characters in the play does not know. Actions, or what people say, can be ironic because the audience see them as having a significance that the characters themselves are unaware of. These are often the moments which make an audience go 'ouch!' Look at the following four instances from the play; then talk about why you think they might be seen as ironic, and how they add to the overall effect of the play.

a David's family give him a cheerful-looking sleeping bag for Christmas.

b Link is brought out of his Caribbean dream by a resonant fart.

c Shelter's choice of a code name for himself and his 'recruits'.

d Gail introducing Link to Gavin as 'the boy I told you about'.

Try to find other examples from the play and say why you think they are ironic.

Things to write about

5 Shelter keeps an audio diary of his 'mission'. Look back over some of his speeches and discuss how the type of language he uses tells us something about him. Pick out particular words and phrases that reveal that he was in the army. This sort of specialist language is called a 'register'.

- Write a speech for Shelter in which he describes another 'mission'.

- Write the letter that he originally sent to the *Daily Tribune*.

In both cases, try to use the same style and register as the character in the play.

6 What is the story that Louise Bains writes? Work in pairs or small groups to produce two different versions:

- the one that she wants, and that she feels she ought, to write;

- the one that Mr Stamp wants in order to catch the eye of more readers.

Talk about the different styles you have used, and the effect you are trying to create.

7 Although *Stone Cold* is a fiction, the truth it is based on is all too real. There are many young homeless people and a shocking number of them do just disappear. Some are certainly murdered.

For a production of this play you might choose to take the opportunity of telling the audience more about the real situation through carefully produced programme notes.

- Look through the section *Life on the Streets* (pages 93–96).

- Use the information there, and any other research you are able to do, to produce a set of programme notes which would inform a theatre audience about homelessness.

8 *Stone Cold* is a very bleak story. Some might say that books and plays such as this are not suitable for young people, precisely because they are so dark. They offer no hope, and show only the worst side of human nature and society. What do you think?

- Jot down arguments both for and against the use of plays like this in schools.

- Use your notes to write an essay which either defends the play or argues why it is unsuitable.

- Imagine that the play is the subject of a debate on TV. Who might be invited to contribute to the debate? Choose four different sorts of people who might have good reason for feeling strongly about the play. Write the debate they have, using the format of a play script.

BRINGING THE PLAY TO LIFE

9 How would Link's mum, sister and Vince react when they read Louise Bains' report of Shelter's murders and see Link's picture in the newspaper? Read through Act One Scenes 3, 5 and 7, and:

- talk about what these scenes reveal about their attitude to David/Link;

- talk about what their attitude to each other seems to be;

- use what you have discovered either to write or to improvise a scene in which Carol enters with a copy of the *Daily Tribune*. Try to find a powerful way of ending the scene.

10 Look back to the end of Act One (Scene 16, pages 51–52) in which the dossers on Captain Hook's barge become a part of Link's dream.

- Work in groups to rehearse the scene. Think about how movement, and the way you use your voices, could make the scene dreamlike. You may choose to add some more lines of your own, or repeat some, to make the scene more effective.

- Imagine that Shelter also has a dream after he has been taken to prison. Invent a 'voice collage', selecting lines from the play or inventing lines of your own, and weaving them together with movement to show Shelter's dream (or is it a nightmare?).

11 Shelter uses a number of clever devices to capture his victims. With Tom, he plays a caring youth worker or hostel worker. He tricks Debs by pretending to be a security officer open to bribery. Ginger is tricked because Shelter knows that he is concerned about Link and would want to help him.

- Look back through the play to remind yourself how the audience is made to realise that Toya and Scouse have also become victims.

- In pairs or groups, devise a scene which shows how he captured these victims.

- Would it be worth including these new scenes into a production of the play? What would they add? Or would they weaken the play in some way?

12 You probably noticed that an audience watching this play is never actually shown Shelter murdering any of his victims.

- Look back through the play and discuss what different techniques the playwright uses to tell the audience that a murder has been committed.

- Discuss why you think Joe Standerline chose these methods rather than actually showing the murders themselves.

- In pairs or small groups, devise another scene which would make it clear to an audience that a murder takes place but does not actually show the crime. Your scene should try to capture the tension and the horror of the event without actually showing the deed itself.

STAGING THE PLAY

13 Shelter's flat is described in some detail at the start of the play (see Act One Scene 2, page 13), yet most of the other scenes are just suggested.

- List all of the different locations mentioned in the play.

- Jot down your ideas about how each of these locations (apart from Shelter's flat) might be suggested by using one or two pieces of 'stage furniture' (for example a litter bin or bus stop), recorded sound or lighting.

- In a live production, what would the benefits be of suggesting scenes in a simple way like this?

- How important would it be to show Shelter's flat in detail? What dramatic effect would the contrast between his flat and the empty street have?

- Think about the performance space in your school. Draw a stage plan showing how you could arrange the space in order to show Shelter's flat *and* all of the other scenes, with as little shifting of scenery as possible.

14 Many of the scenes in this play incorporate flashbacks: things that Link is remembering are brought to life to show the audience what his experience has been. Read through Act One Scene 3 again (pages 14–18). The scene jumps from Link on his own on the street, to a scene in which he meets an old teacher, and then further back in time to a scene before he left home.

- In groups, rehearse this extract.

- Find a way of making what is happening clear to an audience through your use of space and the way you play the characters.

- If you could use lighting and perhaps sound equipment, how might you make it clearer still that the audience are seeing scenes from the past that now only exist in Link's memory?

15 A few specific pieces of music are suggested in the script (for example, Michael Jackson's 'Santa Claus is coming to town' (Act One Scene 5) and Phil Collins' 'Just another day in Paradise' (Act One Scene 12).

- Talk about the dramatic effect these pieces of music would have on an audience.

- Suggest where else music might be used to add to the drama. If you can think of a specific piece of music that would be suitable, explain your choice.

16 Re-read the end of Act Two Scene 10 (pages 77–82). This is the climax of the play. There is a great deal of action and, in a production, the audience will need to understand exactly what is going on if they are to experience tension rather than simply see confusion on stage. Not only does Link almost become another of Shelter's victims and is rescued in the nick of time, but he also discovers Gail's true identity.

- Draw a graph of the scene, showing how the tension rises and falls.

- In groups, rehearse the scene.

- Think about how to show the sudden changes in Shelter's and Gail's attitudes; how important it is to get the timing right so that the audience are brought to the edge of their seats; and how to show Link's change from fear to anger when he learns who Gail is.

LIFE ON THE STREETS

Centrepoint is a charity that was set up specifically to help young homeless people. Over the years they have gathered a great deal of information about why and how young people become homeless, what sort of things can happen to them on the street, and how best to help them. The following facts and extracts are taken from Centrepoint's annual report for 1997:

- Around 43,000 young people are recorded missing each year.

- Nobody actually knows the total number of homeless people, but it is estimated at between 200,000 and 300,000.

- 1 in 20 young people are likely to experience homelessness at some time.

- 78% of runaways under the age of 16 have run away from their family homes.

- One in three young people that Centrepoint deal with have been approached for prostitution. One in five have been approached for drugs.

- One in three of the young homeless suffer from

health problems. Many have chest infections including TB caused by sleeping rough.

Statistics like these are shocking enough, but the actual stories of real people help us understand them better:

When I told my mum my step-dad had raped me, she threw me out. I wanted to sort things out with her but she refused to listen. I knew nothing about being on the streets. I actually had to live in a cardboard box and I managed to get hold of a sleeping bag until some kids set fire to it while I was asleep. I did beg. I didn't care how much people gave me, so long as it was enough to buy something to eat. Some street sleepers were very kind. There's a community spirit.

I've been on and off the streets for three years. I was kicked out by my mum as we weren't getting on so I went to stay with my step-dad. He didn't want me either, and so I had to go. It was Christmas Eve 1994. Out on the streets there's nothing to do. I wouldn't wish it on anyone. You need to be vigilant all the time, especially at night. You see people pointing at you, talking and looking down on you. 'Get a job. Get a life,' they shout.

Sleeping rough is just that... rough. The streets are violent and dangerous. I would never say to other people my age, 'Don't leave home.' Often you have no choice.

My mum and dad don't live together. I don't get on with my step-dad because he hits my mum. I couldn't live with my mum and I couldn't live with my dad, so I had to leave.

One of the biggest problems young homeless people face is the misinformed attitude of many of the general public. For example:

They make loads of money from begging.

In fact, 41% of the young people Centrepoint surveyed had no income at all.

Why can't they just go home?

Many of the young homeless have been pushed out by their families. 20% are evicted or just told to leave. 10% have left to get away from physical or sexual abuse. Others have no family. 17% come from care; once aged 16 or 17, they may be asked by the local authority to leave and look after themselves.

They are workshy. If they had worked harder at school they'd be all right now.

The fact is that 64% of young people on the street have some sort of qualification. Young black people tend to be better qualified than their white counterparts. 90% of those surveyed were either working, in education or training, or actively seeking work. The fact that they were homeless was making it difficult for them to fulfil their ambitions.

If they are on the street, it's probably because they are troublemakers.

Over 80% of young people on the street have never been in trouble with the police.

17 Work in small groups to invent a number of other personal stories of young people who might be found on the street.

- Think about why they had to leave home; how long they have been on the street; what sort of attitudes they have come across from the public; and the best and worst things that have happened to them on the street.

- Write or improvise a monologue in which each character tells the audience their personal story.

- Rather than simply giving one monologue after another, experiment with ways of cutting from one to another and back again to try and make the sequence more interesting to watch and listen to.

18 There are a number of moments in *Stone Cold* which give the audience an insight into what everyday life on the streets is like for young homeless people. For example, when the Policeman moves Ginger and Link on (pages 39–40), or when Ginger tries to teach Link how to 'tap' (pages 41–43). Working in small groups, find a way of using a number of short lines and movements to show 'A Day in the Life of a Dosser'.

19 *I would never say to other people my age, 'Don't leave home.' Often you have no choice.*

- What is your reaction to this statement from a young homeless person? If it really is true that sometimes people have 'no choice' but to leave home, what advice could be given to them about what to do for the best?

- Use your own research and thoughts on this to write or improvise a short 'public information' film designed to inform and help people who feel that their only choice is to leave home.